Channels *of* Peace

How Science *and* Faith
Can Transform Your Family

Samantha Duggan, Ph.D.

For my family

CONTENTS

AUTHOR'S NOTE

THE PRAYER OF ST. FRANCIS

Being a parent is a journey filled with unexpected combinations of joy, struggle, and growth. The challenges are different for all of us, but one thing remains the same—we are constantly stretched in ways we never anticipated. Yet, amid the chaos and uncertainty, there are moments of profound discovery—moments that connect the dots between faith, parenting, and the search for inner peace.

This book is woven from three threads of my life: my spiritual awakening, my experience of parenthood, and my background in psychology. These reflections are anchored in the timeless *Prayer of St. Francis of Assisi**, a prayer I first encountered as a child, humming its melody long after school choir rehearsals. Over the years, it faded from my life until it resurfaced at a moment when I needed it most.

At the time, I was experiencing a deep spiritual shift. In 2007, God turned my life upside down, prompting a spiritual awakening I neither planned for nor expected. At the same time, I was thrown

---

* Though commonly attributed to St. Francis, the origin of this prayer is unknown; it first appeared in print in 1912, over 600 years after his death, and only later became associated with him.

headfirst into the wild terrain of early parenthood. My children were three and one, and I had just transitioned from a full-time career with a supportive nanny to being home with them full-time. It was like stepping onto a new planet without a map.

St. Francis Prayer and Recovery

For me, this spiritual shift took the form of 12-step recovery, a framework that emphasises spiritual growth through principles like prayer, meditation, and service. The *Prayer of St. Francis* became deeply meaningful during this time, as it was used by the founder of Alcoholics Anonymous in *The Twelve Steps and Twelve Traditions* to explain Step 11—seeking conscious contact with God through prayer and meditation. In recovery, meditation doesn't begin with emptying the mind but with reflecting on words that guide us towards spiritual growth. That's exactly what this prayer did for me.

Recovery brought lessons about powerlessness over people, places, and things. But knowing I was powerless didn't magically make bedtime battles or toddler tantrums easier to handle. I was a ball of nerves at times, grasping at spiritual principles while trying to manage squabbles and sleep schedules. Slowly, I began to see these daily struggles as invitations to grow, learn, and connect with my children in ways I never anticipated.

Psychology Meets Practice

As a psychologist, I entered parenthood armed with theory, research, and a head full of scientific knowledge about human behaviour and development. But knowing the *why* didn't help me with the *how*. The gap between what I knew and what I could do left me humbled—and determined to learn.

I immersed myself in new tools, from Non-Violent Communication to trauma-informed approaches and attachment parenting. I trained as a parenting group facilitator and, bit by bit, started applying these insights in real time. My home became a live laboratory where trial and error shaped both my parenting and my personal growth. Parenting, I realised, is an art of experimentation—a risky, messy, beautiful adventure.

Who This Book Is For?

If you're a parent, whether or not you're in recovery, this book is for you. If you're familiar with the prayer of St. Francis, you might find new meaning in its timeless wisdom. If not, I invite you to discover its profound simplicity and depth.

For those who, like me, relate to the prodigal son rather than the older brother in Jesus' parable, this book offers a perspective that embraces imperfection and grace. And if neither of these roles—prodigal or older brother—speaks to you, consider this: it's written from the perspective of a black sheep trying to find its way home.

No matter where you are on your journey, my hope is that you'll find something here—whether encouragement, practical tools, or spiritual nourishment—to help you navigate the complexities of parenting with faith, love, and resilience.

A Note on Language

Words can carry different meanings for each of us. When I speak of *God*, *forgiveness*, or *discipline*, what you hear may not match what I intend. That's the tricky thing about language. I hope your heart will hear what mine is trying to say. Please know that I offer this book with love, trusting that where my words fall short, God will make up the rest.

Parenting is messy, faith is imperfect, and recovery is a winding road. Yet, in all of it, there's grace. This book is my attempt to share what I've learned—take what resonates and leave the rest. Above all, know that you're not alone on this journey.

PROLOGUE

My Shrivelled Heart

Take my heart and make it clean

Open up my eyes to the things unseen

Show me how to love like you have loved me

Hosanna by Brooke Fraser

THE AWAKENING

In 2007, I began a slow and often painful spiritual awakening. God revealed himself unmistakably in my life, and it felt as though I had no choice but to release the grasp of my past and step into something new, something unknown yet strangely hopeful.

Discovering that God was real was an indescribable relief. It was like being handed a map in the middle of a dark wilderness. The stories of my childhood, at least some of them, turned out to be true, though my initial conception of God was anything but clear. At the time, I thought of God as a kind of benevolent Being who cared about me in some vague, abstract way. What I didn't realise then, but came to understand as profoundly significant, was that I had started to think of God as a *who*, rather than as a *what*.

That early understanding gradually evolved into something more concrete: the conscious realisation that God was a divine person, someone who had brought me into being and with whom I could have a relationship. In truth, that relationship had existed all along, but for years, I had been the one neglecting it. When this reality became clear, it felt like a new beginning, as though God and I were reacquainting ourselves after a long separation.

THE IMAGE OF THE HEART

Through this renewed connection, God began to teach me many things about myself. Some of these lessons were sorrowful, others beautiful—many of them brought me to tears. One of the hardest truths he revealed was the state of my heart: it was shrivelled, weak, and incapable of loving fully.

As a child, I had been taught about the purity of a white heart and how sin could stain it, leaving murky grey or charred black marks. I desperately wanted to keep my heart clean, but I inevitably failed. Over time, sadness, guilt, and frustration gave way to indifference, and eventually, I scoffed at the notion entirely, along with much of the theology I'd been raised with.

Now, looking back, I smile at how right those lessons were. The nuns in my school had been trying to teach me something vital for my survival in life. Our hearts, like any muscle, can weaken and shrink when they are not nourished by love. Bitterness, despair, hate, rejection and unforgiveness can starve a heart until it becomes incapable of giving or receiving love. This is not just a personal tragedy; it is a collective one.

THE PATH TO LOVE

As I write these words today, I no longer feel shame admitting I once had a shrivelled heart. It was true then, but it is not true now. God, in his boundless love, reached down into the chaos of my life and rescued me. His love poured into me, expanding my heart so that I could begin to reflect even a fraction of the love he had shown me. He didn't leave me in the mess I had made; instead, he gave me purpose and began healing me.

The most staggering part of this journey is how God chooses to work through flawed, broken people like me. No one is ever useless to God if they are willing to make an effort for him. He took my life, messy and imperfect as it was, and turned it into a co-creation for a single purpose: to expand my heart so that I might love more.

Who do I love now, you might ask? The answer is simple yet infinite: I strive to love God, my husband, my children, my family, my neighbours, my enemies, the world, and yes, myself.

St. Irenaeus, a 2nd-century bishop of Lyons, wrote *The glory of God is man fully alive.* To be fully alive is to love, and this book is the story of how I learned to love—through the grace of God, the challenges of parenting, and the hard work of spiritual growth.

1

Make Me a Channel of Thy Peace

Ever since I was a little girl, I knew I was not one of God's natural saints. Being a channel of peace did not come easily to me. Growing up in Ireland during the 1970s, where children were expected to be seen and not heard, I wasn't particularly outspoken at first. Yet, even then, I often found myself silently questioning what I heard and what I was told.

In the place and time I grew up, adults were treated with the utmost respect, and their authority was rarely challenged. Part of me looked forward to the day when I would be an adult. Without ever putting this thought into words, I sensed that someday I wouldn't have to be quiet anymore. What I didn't anticipate was just how loud I would become—and how soon.

By the time I was eleven or twelve, I had started speaking up in situations where many others couldn't or wouldn't, and by adulthood, it had become second nature. In some ways, this is a gift for which I am deeply grateful, but in others, it is a curse.

Speaking out at inopportune times often landed me in trouble at school, where teachers of the time had little tolerance for pupils who challenged them.

THE POWER AND PITFALLS OF SPEAKING OUT

Looking back, it's striking how unusual it was for a twelve-year-old schoolgirl in those days to criticise a teacher's methods. Yet there I was, voicing opinions on everything from the criteria for classroom streaming to the way hockey practices were run. These are not exaggerated examples but real-life events—specific memories that underline how I was anything but a channel of God's peace at that age.

Even now, I see both the gift and the curse of my tendency to speak out. On the one hand, history shows us that progress often comes from people who are willing to challenge the status quo. Whether it's standing against the mistreatment of women and children, fighting for the education of all people regardless of race, gender, or ability, or opposing modern-day slavery, it is often the disagreeable voices that say, *No more*. These are the voices that disrupt injustice and demand change, and I'm grateful to be part of that tradition.

Disagreeable people, though, those who are unafraid to disagree and speak their minds, are not obvious peacemakers.

Quite the opposite—they tend to generate conflict. People like me wade into conversations others would avoid, unafraid to challenge even the aggressive or forceful. While I might find such interactions unsettling in hindsight, they don't stop me from speaking up in the moment.

It would be easy to assume I'm an extrovert, but in reality, I'm a sociable introvert—a person who finds people fascinating yet draining. I love lively conversations but need time alone to recharge. My instinctive shyness doesn't diminish my urge to speak out when I feel strongly, but it creates a dichotomy that I've had to learn to live with. I've come to believe that this tension between quiet introspection and outspoken conviction was given to me for a purpose. Accepting it hasn't always been easy, but it has been part of my journey towards understanding who I am and what I'm meant to do.

TO SPEAK UP OR HOLD YOUR SILENCE?

I've learned that just because my tendency to disagree arises in certain situations, it doesn't mean I always have to voice it. One of the most valuable things I was ever taught was to ask myself three simple questions before speaking up: *Does it need to be said? Does it need to be said now? Does it need to be said now by me?*

Answering these questions usually gives me the clarity I need to decide whether to speak or hold my silence.

Learning to bite my tongue using this mantra has been transformative. Not only has it improved my relationships, but it's also helped me feel more at ease with others in general. After all, being the person who says the uncomfortable thing can sometimes make you the person others don't know quite what to do with—admired from a distance but rarely the first on anyone's invitation list.

I've come to realise that while some people might quietly appreciate someone who speaks up, they often keep that appreciation to themselves. Plenty of others, of course, would much rather dismiss the message entirely and the messenger while they're at it. And honestly, I don't blame them. Most people don't enjoy conflict. Who wants to be around someone who always seems ready to start a debate? Or sit next to the parent on the committee who raises objections to everything? And let's face it, how many people will gravitate towards the mum who admits to believing in God or suggests that sex outside marriage might not be the best idea? Let's just say, not many.

PRIORITISING PERSONAL PEACE

These days, I reserve my true thoughts for close friends. For acquaintances, I present a more measured version of myself. While I once believed radical openness was the key to connection, I've learned it often has the opposite effect. Oversharing left me feeling exposed and ashamed, creating distance between myself and others.

For years, I struggled with a part of myself I didn't fully understand. I thought of it as my *mouthy* side, always ready with a sharp word or defiant comment. I blamed this part of me for misunderstandings and conflict, for moments when I longed for connection but instead created distance. At first, this seemed irrational—why would I push people away when I wanted a connection? But then I remembered something from my psychological training: we often repeat harmful patterns because they feel familiar, even comforting. My identity as a funny but mouthy outsider, someone unafraid to speak her mind, had become a habit I clung to, even when it no longer served me.

It wasn't until I began exploring the concept of the *Inner Child* that the pieces started to fall into place. As I tentatively began imagining conversations with different parts of myself, I uncovered something unexpected. I realised this outspoken, defiant part of me wasn't just a flaw; it was a younger part of me, shaped by years of needing to be bold and protective. When I finally understood this, something shifted. I began to see that this part of me had been doing her best to help me, even her methods sometimes backfired.

Calling her Janey gave me a way to connect with her, to understand her boldness as something that had once kept me safe but now needed a gentler approach. This shift helped me move from resentment to appreciation, and I realised that making peace with Janey was essential to finding peace within myself. Learning when to let her speak and when to guide her gently became a cornerstone of my personal growth. It taught me how to foster calm rather than conflict and connection rather than distance. Living in harmony with Janey has helped me become the person I aspire to be, someone who brings peace into every area of life, starting from within.

FINDING JANEY

It was an older, wiser friend who encouraged me to engage my inner children more deeply. Sceptical at first, I tried to approach the process with curiosity rather than contempt. One day, as I imagined a conversation with a younger part of myself, she introduced herself as Janey. The name surprised me—my name is Samantha Marie—but then I remembered how a favourite aunt used to call me Sammy-Jane as a child. Suddenly, this process of self-discovery didn't seem so absurd.

At first, Janey appeared as a quiet, cooperative seven-year-old. But soon, a more rebellious figure emerged: a 19-year-old Janey, brash and unapologetic. In my mind, I saw her clearly—cigarette in one hand, glass of red wine in the other, radiating confidence and convinced she was always right. Sober me found her embarrassing, but I couldn't deny her courage and strength. I struggled with the shame of identifying with her bold, unruly nature and the trouble that it sometimes caused.

During this time, I was attending a 12-step fellowship for emotional healing, where we often discussed treating our inner children with gentleness. Many of the other women described wrapping their inner child in a soft blanket as a comforting gesture, so I decided to try the same. After a heated argument with my husband, I realised it wasn't the adult me who was yelling—it was 19-year-old Janey. Taking a moment to calm down, I tentatively imagined offering her a soft blanket. Her response was immediate: a withering glare and a stream of profanity that could make a sailor blush.

Embarrassed but undeterred, I tried something else. I offered her a cigarette instead. She accepted. Without a word, she sat beside me, and for the first time, we were at peace. That small gesture of understanding—an inspired willingness to meet her on her terms—changed everything. From that day forward, Janey began to trust me.

Our relationship grew from there. With time, she felt safe enough to stay silent when I asked. That shift marked a turning point—not just with Janey, but with me. In embracing her, I began to embrace all of me, finding a balance between boldness and peace, defiance and discretion. It wasn't about silencing Janey but about learning to live in harmony with her.

THE PAIN OF SILENCE IN TRAGEDY

While learning when to stay quiet has brought me greater peace, I've also witnessed the pain that too much silence can bring in moments of deep tragedy. Previously, I would look at people who seemed naturally agreeable and wish I were more like them. These days, I better understand that agreeable people have their own challenges.

One of the most agreeable people I've ever known was my school friend, Fiona (not her real name). No matter what was going on around her, Fiona was unfailingly polite and kind to friends, strangers, parents, teachers, younger girls and older girls. She got on with everyone. She had many positive qualities and the whole school thought she was lovely. To me, she seemed faultless. Of course, this was probably unfair to Fiona. If I'd seen her on the inside, I'm sure I'd have noticed struggles like anyone else, but outwardly, this was how she seemed.

Shortly before we became very close, Fiona's family suffered an unspeakable tragedy. Her older brother was killed in a horrific accident, struck by a car while walking home from a friend's house. The whole community was shocked.

I vividly remember the day Sr Thérèse, our French teacher, addressed the tragedy in class. She expressed her condolences to Fiona, mentioning her loss directly. Afterwards, some girls said Fiona had gone to the toilets to cry, and they criticised the nun for bringing it up. They felt it had upset Fiona unnecessarily, and the consensus seemed to be that mentioning the accident had been wrong.

I wasn't sure I agreed. To me, it felt worse to say nothing, pretending this terrible loss hadn't happened. But I stayed quiet, afraid to admit I'd felt relief when Sr Thérèse broke the silence. For a moment, it felt like a weight had been lifted, as though someone had finally said what we were all thinking. Still, I didn't speak up for the nun—she was unpopular, and I didn't want to risk alienating myself. I wondered if the others were right and if I was wrong. Back then, I didn't have enough experience with death to trust my instincts.

Later that year, another girl in our year group lost her younger brother. We were told it was an accident; he'd been playing with a rope and a chair. Tragically, he'd accidentally hanged himself. Everyone knew eleven-year-olds don't kill themselves, but we also knew better than to ask any questions.

It was Ireland in 1985, and our community dealt with this tragedy the same way we had the previous one: by saying nothing. No one knew what to say in the face of such profound loss, so we stayed silent.

CHOOSING KINDNESS AND COMPASSION

I learned many years later that avoiding difficult or awkward topics is sometimes referred to as the *Don't Speak* rule. There is wisdom in this rule if applied in the right measure. Why would one speak in the face of unspeakable tragedy? What can you possibly say when someone is enduring the unimaginable? Yet often, saying nothing creates pain and confusion—the very opposite of peace. Worse still, it does nothing to teach or model compassion.

The Bible offers instruction about how a follower of Christ is meant to behave, particularly in times of crisis. In the letters of St. Paul, he tells the early Christians to clothe themselves with *compassion, kindness, humility, meekness, and patience* and to *bear with one another and, if anyone has a complaint against another, forgive each other.* The Bible, I have found, is often very good at telling us *what* to do but less explicit about *how* to achieve it in practice. For a long time, this left me feeling unsure about how to live up to these ideals.

In our largely secular world today, I find we are much the same. We are very concerned with teaching our children to be kind, but are we succeeding? We tell them *what* to be, but do we teach them *how* to become it?

Words are one of the most powerful tools we have for expressing kindness and compassion, yet they often seem to fail us. This is why I love watching television dramas set in the past, like *Downton Abbey* or *Poldark.* In these shows, the characters often seem more adept at navigating difficult conversations than we are today. For example, in a series about Queen Victoria, there is an episode where Prince Albert discovers that his brother, Ernst, has been secretly suffering from syphilis, a result of a reckless trip to Paris after their father's death. When Ernst finally confesses his illness to Albert, they share this exchange:

Albert: "Why didn't you tell me?"

Ernst: "I was ashamed."

Then they hug and cry. How beautiful. How simple, yet how difficult. Are we this skilful at speaking about hard things today? I doubt it. We are frequently told to *have a conversation* about challenging topics, like mental health, but the advice often stops there. Beyond saying, *We need to talk about this*, we rarely go any further.

Of course, these dramas are scripted, and we can't assume they reflect exactly how people spoke in those times. But even imagining that people once expressed themselves with such skill and sensitivity offers us lessons for today. I often notice small phrases that seem just the right thing to say—expressions I've never heard spoken in real life. For example, *I am much obliged.* While this might feel overly formal today, it could easily be updated to *I'm very grateful,* or *I appreciate that* without losing any of its warmth or sincerity. It's a reminder that the words we choose can carry immense weight and, when spoken with care, have the power to build bridges of kindness and compassion.

THE COMPLEXITIES OF PRAISE AND APPRECIATION

By way of illustration, let me tell a story. I once recommended a book to a parenting group I was leading. Afterwards, one of the parents texted me, asking for the title. When I got home, I took a photo of the book and sent it to him, along with a couple of lines about why I recommended it. His reply was ostensibly gracious: "You're very kind".

On the surface, this was a polite response. But the truth is, it irked me. You might wonder why. It's because his comment was about me, not him. It broke the golden rule of using *I statements* to speak about oneself instead of *you statements* about others.

Some people might like being told they're kind, but I wasn't particularly impressed by my kindness in this instance—I had simply sent a photo and a text. Jesus himself said: *Being kind to people who are kind to you isn't exceptional; even the Gentiles do that* (adapted from Matthew 5:46–47). My internal response was a snort: *I'm not an especially kind person, and anyone who thinks I am, has set the bar rather low.*

What would have been better? I would have preferred if he had texted, *I appreciate that*, or simply, *thank you.* Then I could have replied, *You're welcome*, and that would have been that. Of course, the man who sent the text had no idea that I'd struggled with praise. But I've noticed I'm not alone. Many people—women especially—tend to deflect compliments, often brushing them away with suspicion or disbelief.

PRAISE AND CRITICISM IN PRACTICE

In the parenting classes I lead, we do an exercise that reveals how people feel about praise and criticism. Participants write down a few words about how they feel when they receive praise. Most responses are positive—*encouraged, happy, motivated*—but there are always a few wary ones: *suspicious*, *disbelieving*, or *worried—what do they want?*

We then discuss how these reactions often stem from childhood experiences. People who were starved of praise as children can find it difficult to accept as adults, much like pouring water onto a dried-up sponge. To illustrate this, we perform an exercise: we pour a large quantity of water onto a dry sponge and watch it bounce off. Then, we slowly drip water onto another dry sponge, showing how steady, gradual encouragement is more effective.

The same principle applies to praise. Individuals unaccustomed to compliments often reject them, but a slow and steady approach—understated compliments and consistent appreciation—can help them grow more comfortable over time.

On the whole, I find it safer and more effective to express gratitude or appreciation rather than give compliments. Appreciation creates a positive glow in people, including children, when their efforts are recognised. It also has the wonderful side effect of making the person expressing gratitude feel more positive, grateful and connected.

Becoming Generous

Expressing gratitude has had unexpected benefits for me. When my husband and I first married, our biggest argument in the first year was about saying thank you. He believed in expressing gratitude for even small gestures, like bringing a glass of water. I, on the other hand, thought my gratitude should be assumed. He insisted it wasn't enough to feel grateful—I had to say it out loud.

At the time, I thought his stance was childish. Over time, I realised he was right. Saying thank you not only strengthened our relationship but also changed me. These days, I like to think I've become a genuinely grateful person because I've made a habit of noticing what others do for me and expressing appreciation.

I've also learned to embrace different kinds of gratitude. Even when I don't particularly like a gift, I can still be thankful for the thought and effort behind it. Gratitude, I've come to see, is about more than merely liking a gift—it's about recognising the value of care and kindness; however, it comes.

These lessons in generosity and honesty apply just as much to my relationship with my children. By modelling gratitude and expressing appreciation, I hope to teach them how to channel peace in their own lives, even in small ways.

What's our baseline for being a kind and generous person? Christianity sets a high one: *Be perfect, therefore, as your heavenly Father is perfect* (Matthew 5:48). Modern translations often shy away from the word perfect, and for good reason—it's a standard most of us can't hope to meet. But that's the point: we need God's grace to approach it.

Still, what would it look like if we all tried to be more perfectly generous? Would a generous person bring a gift every time they visit someone's house, even for a quick coffee? Perhaps not. But what about bringing a small gift when invited for a meal? To me, that feels like a reasonable baseline, though it's not the only valid one.

I wasn't always someone who brought gifts. But, after listening to Deepak Chopra's *Seven Spiritual Laws of Success*, I was struck by the idea of always bringing something when visiting someone's home. Chopra suggests the gift need not be extravagant—it could be as simple as a prayer or a single flower. The point isn't the item but the spirit of generosity. This idea resonated deeply with me, and I vowed to make it part of my life.

This simple practice has been a great spiritual teacher. Still, I haven't managed to follow it perfectly. Sometimes, I don't want to bother bringing a gift, especially when visiting someone who doesn't bring me anything in return. In those moments, I remind myself that true generosity asks us to give without expecting anything back.

When I find myself resenting the act of giving, I know I'm being transactional rather than generous. In those moments, the best spiritual progress is not in forcing myself to bring a gift but in bringing myself honestly, without resentment. I've learned that doing something begrudgingly, no matter how well-intentioned, is the opposite of being a channel of God's peace.

This lesson applies beyond gift-giving. I know I'm not gracious enough to do things I truly hate without resenting them later. If my husband suggests something adventurous, like stand-up paddle boarding, I've realised it's more generous to say no upfront than to agree and then ruin the experience for both of us.

Final Reflections on Peace

Peace begins as an internal choice, a deliberate effort to understand and embrace the different parts of ourselves, even those we once resented. By making peace within, we create space for kindness, compassion, and gratitude to flourish, not as ideals to strive towards but as natural extensions of who we are.

For some, this journey may involve finding the courage to speak up rather than staying silent. For others, it means choosing silence over sharp words. For me, it's meant learning how to discern between each of these. All these paths require self-awareness and compassion, and both lead us closer to a sense of calm and harmony within ourselves and with those around us.

When we thoughtfully choose our words or embrace silence, we honour not only our own boundaries but also the emotional landscapes of others. These small, intentional acts—expressing gratitude, softening in moments of conflict, and showing compassion even when it's difficult—ripple outward, shaping our relationships and our communities.

Though we may never fully embody the ideals of our faith or our highest aspirations, every effort matters. Every moment of understanding, every step towards connection, brings us closer to the life we long for: one that is rich in meaning, anchored in love, and capable of transforming the world around us.

2

Where There Is Hatred, Let Me Bring Love

Every parent, at some point, faces a child grappling with self-doubt—or even self-hatred. For much of my life, I assumed this was uncommon, but with time, I've come to believe that no one escapes some degree of self-rejection. Still, I was surprised when I saw it in my own children, as I lacked the wisdom to understand it then.

My son wasn't yet two and a half when I first saw something in him that resembled self-denigration. I felt a wave of guilt and assumed his shame was my fault. Surely, I thought, it must stem from mistakes my husband and I had made in parenting him.

I remember the moment vividly. We were in the kitchen, and I had lifted Flynn onto the counter, perhaps after some minor infraction like refusing lunch or deliberately dropping food. My intention, as I recall, was to put us on the same level and explain calmly why his behaviour wasn't acceptable. Before I could begin, however, he looked up at me and said, "Flynn bad".

I was shocked and panicked. How could he think that about himself when I had worked so hard to separate the act from the actor? I had tried to make it clear that it was his behaviour, not his person, that was the issue. Yet it became obvious that this distinction was beyond him. Looking back, I can see I wasn't just reacting to his pain—I was responding to something unresolved in myself. His shame echoed something ancient and familiar in me, though I didn't yet have the words for it.

Right then, I resolved to change the way I was parenting. I had (so I thought) undeniable evidence that my approach wasn't working. He felt ashamed when I corrected him. Like many parents of my generation, I treated shaming one's child as the ultimate sin, leaving me feeling constrained when it came to discipline. I wanted to correct Flynn's behaviour without causing self-reproach, but this left me relying almost entirely on reasoning and explanations to manage his inevitable toddler mischief.

Without realising it, I was practising *Gentle Parenting* long before it became a popular term. I believed if Flynn could understand what I wanted him to do—or stop doing—he would comply naturally. This approach also aligned with my then-worldview. I had distanced myself from the Christian idea of humanity's tendency towards wrongdoing and embraced the humanist belief that people are intrinsically good. I was convinced that my son would grow into a kind and virtuous person as long as I didn't damage him with clumsy parenting.

Once I became a mother, it was almost inevitable that I would turn the same critical eye on myself that I had once cast on my parents. Seeing my toddler son struggling with shame, I assumed that his feelings must stem from my parenting mistakes. Driven by guilt, I resolved to change my approach entirely, determined to undo whatever harm I thought I had caused. I worked hard to demonstrate more patience, believing this would help him feel safe and loved. I thought I was doing the right thing—choosing patience over punishment—but in hindsight, I was avoiding discomfort, not modelling emotional maturity.

Yet, in my effort to be endlessly patient, I found myself suppressing my true feelings. When his behaviour irritated or frustrated me, I ignored it, convincing myself to rise above my emotions. But the emotions didn't disappear; they simply built up, unchecked, until the weight of all the small, unaddressed frustrations burst forth in an eruption of anger, completely disproportionate to the moment at hand. This cycle was not good for him, for me, or for our family. Suppressed emotions always find a way out, and the way they emerge is rarely kind or loving.

My outbursts had far-reaching consequences that I never intended. They frightened my son, strained our relationship, failed to teach him the lessons I wanted him to learn, and left me grappling with an overwhelming sense of parental shame once my anger had subsided.

TEACHING BY EXAMPLE

At the time, I didn't understand that a natural sense of shame plays a vital role in the development of conscience. I also didn't realise that my son needed me to correct him calmly and consistently at the moment when he stepped out of line. I lacked the tools to address his behaviour constructively—I didn't know how to deliver corrections with a matter-of-fact tone, use consequences effectively, or empathise with his inevitable frustration over boundaries.

Worse, I didn't see how my inability to stay emotionally close to him while disciplining was undermining our connection. I failed to appreciate that I could guide him to respect limits without severing the relationship we both needed. Like all toddlers, he was testing boundaries and learning the rules of the world. But instead of responding with calm resolve and setting effective boundaries, I fell back on reasoning, requests, and explanations that failed to reach him. This eventually led to frustration and anger, as I remained unaware of how deeply my own unresolved self-hatred was interfering with my ability to parent with love.

I had to learn the hard way that being a truly loving parent is impossible when you are burdened by self-loathing. It is a spiritual axiom—an undeniable truth: you cannot pass on what you do not possess. If you lack a deep and secure sense of your own worth, free from guilt, shame, and self-rejection, no matter how much you want to, you cannot instil a secure sense of self-worth in your child. I didn't just need better parenting strategies—I needed healing.

It's true that an intellectual understanding of our immense value, as beloved children of our Creator, the Universe, or the source of all love, can be shared, and this is a meaningful and positive step. However, knowing this truth in your mind is vastly different from feeling it in your heart. Knowing it in your head might guide your words, but feeling it in your heart is what truly shapes the love you embody and pass on.

TO BE LOVED IS TO BE HEALED

Christian doctrine teaches that we are loved by God—a theological fact that many of us accept as head knowledge. But there's another kind of knowing, one that is profoundly different. It's the knowledge you carry deep in your soul, written on your heart: you can know you are loved by God because you have felt it, experienced it, and had it revealed to you.

I became a much more loving parent when I started to believe in God again. But my capacity to love leapt forward when I realised I was God's beloved. Suddenly, the meaning of familiar Christian texts crystallised: we love because we are first loved.

As a teenager, I thought this language was poetic, even pretty, but I didn't truly comprehend it. Although I understood the words themselves, I glossed over them, dimly aware that their full meaning eluded me. Eventually, I decided it was just theological nonsense, a proposition too abstract to make a difference. What I didn't realise at the time was that my misunderstanding reflected a deeper reality: I didn't truly believe I was loved by God.

His Favour Rests on Us All

Many years later, I read Henri Nouwen's *Life of the Beloved,* and just as I vividly remember the first time Flynn verbalised his self-rejection, I have a stark memory of the moment the truth of my beloved-ness began to sink in.

I was raised on the translation: *This is my beloved Son, in whom I am well pleased* (Matthew 3:17). It always seemed to imply a conditional love, dependent on performance. Of course, Jesus—the perfect God-man—would elicit God's pleasure. But how could my own rather miserable performance, my many failures, procrastination, lapses in judgement, and downright sinfulness, ever merit the approval of almighty God?

When I read Nouwen's version—*This is my beloved Son, on whom my favour rests*—it stopped me in my tracks. It wasn't about earning God's love; his favour simply rested on Jesus. Before his ministry had even begun, before he had done anything at all, God declared him beloved.

At that moment, something in me shifted. These words applied not only to Jesus but to me, too. For the first time, I understood what it meant to be loved without condition, without achievement or perfection. It didn't require performance; it was simply true.

TRAVERSING THE GRIEF OF LETTING GO

I was sitting in a pub in the middle of the day when I read those words, and suddenly, God's love burned into my heart, my soul, and my mind. Tears poured down my face as I realised how many years I had spent not knowing this truth.

How different would life have been if I had always known it? If I had believed this earlier, especially before my children were born? The regret hit me like a tidal wave. *Please, God,* I prayed, *why couldn't I have known this before?*

In retrospect, I see now that I was grieving—grieving the lost years, the missed opportunities to live in the light of God's love. Though I knew intellectually about Elisabeth Kübler-Ross's stages of grief, including the bargaining phase, I didn't recognise it in myself at the time. I only knew that I was pleading with God, aching to understand why it couldn't have been different. Why had I spent so much of my life not knowing the simple, unshakeable truth of his love?

This bargaining, this mourning of what could have been, was excruciating. Yet, even in the midst of it, God's love was working in me, beginning to heal the wounds left by my years of self-rejection.

NEW BEGINNINGS

The silver lining to all this painful repentance was that I had finally come to understand how precious I was. My mere existence meant that I was loved beyond measure by the God who saw fit to create me. At first, I couldn't see how my awareness of God's immense love for me would begin to melt away years of shame, but over time, it became clear. My sense of shame and self-loathing began to recede slowly but unmistakably.

I didn't know in advance that being freed from self-hatred would enable me to convey self-worth to my children, but as things unfolded, I began to understand. Having a deep and abiding sense of my own self-worth helped me to distinguish which of my children's behaviours needed guidance and what could simply be accepted.

Previously, I had been so concerned with accepting all of their feelings, because mine had been denied during childhood, that I couldn't see the need for limits. Now, I could discern that some feelings could be embraced as they were, while others needed gentle boundaries to protect my children and those around them.

The slow journey to sow love where there had been hatred had begun in earnest. And as my shame lifted, something else began to dissolve: the sense of intense ugliness that had plagued me since my early teens. Knowing that I was loved by the God of the Universe made me feel significant—and, yes, even beautiful.

When you feel God smiling at you, when you truly grasp that he loves you more than you can imagine, it's hard to sustain the perception of being ugly and unworthy. God's love surpasses anything we can fathom, and it is offered so perfectly because, well, he's God.

LETTING GO OF THE HATE

I stopped believing I was ugly and stopped wishing I could be more attractive. No longer did I collapse in tears after haircuts, convinced they emphasised my flaws. But the healing didn't come without pain. There were many, many bouts of what I came to call *snot-crying*. Letting myself feel the raw self-hatred—unadorned by anger or self-pity—was excruciating, but it was also liberating.

I mastered the art of bringing God with me into my cave of shame, where I had been marinating for years. The first time I fell into his arms and let the tears come, it felt as though they would never stop. I grieved for all the years I had lived in self-loathing, unaware that there was another way.

More than grief, though, there was repentance. I wept for how I had done this to myself. Yes, my childhood and family of origin explained much about how I came to feel unworthy. But God showed me that, for most of my life, I had been my own worst enemy.

I didn't need external criticism—I had castigated, rebuked, and hated myself far more than anyone else ever had. Over the years, I had become a relentless critic, but now, God was asking me to let go of the hate.

I've heard it said that God uses our brokenness to help others who have suffered similar wounds. These days, I see people struggling with self-hatred everywhere, and instead of recoiling, I feel compassion.

Previously, I might have responded to rude, impatient, or unkind people with dislike or mistrust. Sometimes—God forgive me—I even hated them. I came to think of this as *committing thought crimes* against others, and by doing so, I added to the hatred in the world. If anyone needed to know that God is merciful and forgives sin, it was me.

But the greatest gift of being freed from self-hatred is how it transformed my ability to respond to my children when they struggled with shame, unworthiness, or self-rejection.

RECLAIMING BEAUTY

I was horrified and saddened the first time my daughter confided in me about feeling ugly. She was so young, only around nine years old, when she first shared her pain. It shocked me to my core, not least because I had been slightly older, about eleven, when I became convinced of my own ugliness.

Thankfully, this conversation came after my pivotal spiritual experiences about my own self-perception. As a result, I was able to listen to her without spiralling into panic or confusion about how to respond. I'm certain that if this had happened before my healing, I would have been far less useful to her.

When we are deeply wounded ourselves, we're too easily triggered into self-centredness to provide the support others need, especially our children. As I listened to her, I was struck by the certainty in her voice. She truly believed she was ugly. Her conviction brought back vivid memories of my own certainty about my supposed ugliness, and I thought, *So I really wasn't making it up: it is possible for someone to REALLY believe they are ugly.*

The heartbreaking thing is that my daughter is not ugly—not even close. She has sparkling green eyes, gorgeous brown curls, and a heart-shaped face that people often compare to a young Emma Watson. Yet despite such compliments, her feelings of ugliness persisted for many years.

Over time, I watched her grow. Her sense of self-worth gradually deepened, and with it, her belief in her own beauty began to take root. Now, as a confident and beautiful young woman, she is not without the occasional hang-up, but she is far from the brokenness I carried at her age. Still, I know from bitter experience that feelings of unworthiness and self-rejection can remain deeply entrenched. They don't sit quietly on the surface; when they rise, they are powerful, and they cannot be banished with platitudes or well-meaning reassurances like *That's not true! But you're so pretty!* Or *don't say that!*

RESPONDING WITH LOVE, NOT FEAR

As a parent, it breaks my heart to hear how often others respond to their children's pain with these kinds of phrases. Let's call the first two *dismiss and deny,* and the third *disapprove*. These reactions are common, but they are deeply unhelpful.

I understand why parents say these things. They aren't trying to hurt their children; they genuinely believe their child is beautiful and are expressing their shock and disbelief. But often, these words also reveal a parent's fear.

When a parent says something like *Don't think that about yourself!* Or *That's not true!* they may be reacting to inner thoughts like, *I don't know how to handle this,* or even fears for a child of depression or self-harm. Fear can make us desperate to fix things quickly, and it often drives us to dismiss or disapprove of what we hear.

Most of us struggle to sit with negative feelings, whether our own or someone else's. Sadness, shame, and self-hatred make us uncomfortable, and so we instinctively try to make them go away.

But this can backfire terribly. Instead of comforting, we may inadvertently teach our children to mistrust both their feelings and us.

BREAKING GENERATIONAL PATTERNS

This dynamic may help explain the heartbreaking distance that often grows between parents and their adult children. I suspect that if we could hear recordings from the past, we'd find many interactions where parents responded to their children from a place of fear rather than love. Over time, these small, unintended wounds accumulate, leaving children feeling unseen and misunderstood.

The tragedy is that these parents loved their children deeply, but didn't know how to express it in a way that truly connected. They acted on fear without realising it or being aware of its long-term consequences.

Breaking this cycle requires courage and intention. When my daughter came to me with her pain, I knew I had to respond differently. I had to draw on my own healing journey to provide her with the love, empathy, and reassurance that I hadn't always received.

STRATEGIES FOR TEACHING LOVE

I hope that now you've stopped and thought about it, you can see why many commonplace strategies fail to teach a child to love instead of hate. This doesn't mean there's no merit in shutting down expressions of hatred in your home or that you must get your words exactly right every time you interact with your child. But if a child declares they hate you, their other parent, a sibling, or even themselves, dismissing their words with phrases like *You don't mean that* or *Don't say that* won't lead to long-term success for your relationship or your child's growth.

Why not? Because those responses contradict the child's experience. In psychological terms, they minimise, deny, or dismiss the child's reality. This approach is easily corrected when you know how. Acknowledge the reality before correcting the behaviour and defining the limit. For example:

I can see you're furious with your dad because he turned off the television after you didn't listen to him. But we don't say 'hate' in this house. You can say you're mad at Dad instead. That's more honest anyway.

This simple adjustment allows your child to feel understood while also teaching them healthier ways to express their emotions. I call it *empathy before education*. When my daughter had moments of self-doubt, convinced she was the worst or not pretty,

I followed this principle: I listened first, nodding, making small noises to show I understood her sadness, before carefully and gently sharing my perspective:

You know, it's not true, even if it feels very real right now. You're actually very lovely and deeply loved.

I would sometimes remind her not just of my love but also of her dad's, her brother's (even when she doubted it), and most importantly, God's. But I never rushed to this part, and I didn't say it every time. If you bring it up too quickly or mention it too often, your child may feel you don't truly understand them. Your silent listening is the empathy part; it's the foundation for everything else.

I also made a conscious effort never to say anything like *I wish you didn't feel like this,* or *Why do you feel like this?* While I often wished she didn't feel like this, or wondered why she did, saying so might have discouraged her from sharing her struggles with me. Questions like *Why?* can unintentionally shut down communication, as they may make a child feel criticised or pressured to explain emotions they can't yet articulate. It's agonising to watch your child suffer, but we must balance our desire to make the pain go away with the ability to sit with them in their suffering.

TEACHING PEACE IN THE STORM

Of course, there are times when it's right to act immediately—removing a splinter, ending the piano lessons, or switching schools. However, with emotional pain, the most loving response is often to let your child feel their emotions first. You might admit you've felt similar things and guide them towards healthy ways of managing their feelings. This is how we bring love where there is hate.

Anger, frustration, and even hatred are part of the human experience, including for children. While some children are mild and easy-going, others have temperaments that are more intense, sensitive, or disagreeable. These children may feel big, angry emotions frequently. For them, it's crucial to learn that while those feelings are natural, they must also learn self-control.

Teaching self-control is best begun early. A two-year-old's tantrum is much easier to manage than that of an older child. If necessary, careful physical restraint might be required for younger children having full-blown tantrums. Starting young prevents neural patterns of unrestrained anger from becoming deeply entrenched, making later self-regulation much harder. Without intervention, a child prone to intense anger may grow into a teenager in deep pain, causing suffering for themselves and others.

I know this first-hand. My daughter, when she was small, was prone to intense tantrums and acting out her rage. I didn't know how to handle it at first, and by the time I learned, I sometimes had to physically restrain her during these episodes. By restraining her gently but firmly, I showed her that I wasn't afraid of her emotions—and that she didn't need to be, either. My calm presence taught her that her big feelings couldn't make me disappear and that she could begin to take charge of herself rather than letting her emotions control her or our household. I regret not knowing earlier how to balance love with boundaries.

Renowned psychologist Jordan Peterson offers an excellent example of teaching self-control early. He describes his own son wrestling with defiance and anger as a toddler, but learning to master those tendencies through consistent boundaries. Physical restraint wasn't needed because Peterson began teaching limits from the start.

I came to understand the importance of these lessons later in my parenting journey. My children suffered from my lack of knowledge, my weaknesses, and my own unresolved issues. Yet, through God's grace, I learned to let go of regret and self-pity and instead cultivate gratitude for the healing that has taken place.

FROM HATRED TO LOVE

Healing often comes with a companion: sorrow for the years we lived without it. But sorrow is not the end of the story. As I reflect now, I can still feel slightly wistful for my daughter's early years, which were more painful than they needed to be. How different might her life have been if I had healed my self-hatred before she was born? I'll never know. I do know we made it through, and I've come to understand the beauty of gratitude over regret.

Where there was once hatred towards me, others, and even life itself, God has brought love. I eventually learned that God loved me, and because he loved me, I learned to love myself. And when I loved myself better, I found I could love others better too.

3

Where There Is Injury, Let Me Bring Pardon

Years ago, a colleague told me how impressed she'd been by a friend's handling of a recent fallout between her son and his best friend. The boys were about eight, and while the offence might seem minor to an adult, it was not so in the eyes of her son. His beloved football team had been insulted, his favourite player mocked, and to make matters worse, his best friend had started to buddy up with another boy who shared this scornful view. To her son, it felt like a terrible betrayal.

The mother understood completely. She knew the hurt was real, even if it didn't require discipline or a meeting with the school. This wasn't a matter for intervention, but it mattered. It was the kind of thing parents used to dismiss with a breezy *Don't let it bother you* or *Boys will be boys*. I'd say that kind of brush-it-off response is far less common now than it once was.

NOT EVERY HURT NEEDS A HERO

In my years as a parent of young children—and witness to many a playground dispute—it seemed to me that a great many parents were now inclined to involve teachers in their child's friendship troubles, or even to raise the issue directly with the other parent. That wasn't how things were done when I was growing up. Back then, I suspect most parents would have simply let the children sort it out themselves.

Of course, these modern parental interventions are usually well-intentioned. Often, parents are simply at a loss—they want to help their child but don't quite know how. Many of us never learned how to offer empathy and guidance without either minimising the hurt or escalating the drama.

Sadly, an adult stepping in can make things worse. Teachers and parents can easily get drawn into the emotional tangle. Things escalate, sides are taken, and *he said, she said* begins—while the children themselves have already made up and moved on in the playground.

Then there are parents who respond to playground disputes by categorising people: nice people like us, and nasty people like your so-called friend. I always wince when I hear a parent say their child, who is so kind and would never hurt anyone, simply can't understand why others are so mean.

I wince not because I doubt their child is lovely, but because I see the trap. These narratives feel comforting—they offer an explanation and give a child permission to feel hurt without shame. But they teach a deeply unhelpful view of the world: that some people are good, and some people are bad. Full stop.

And yet, this is a real difficulty—parents *do* have to teach children about right and wrong, and that there *is* such a thing as badness and even evil in the world. It's not simple. It's a thorny task, trying to help a child develop moral clarity without falling into the trap of moral superiority. We want them to recognise cruelty or betrayal when they see it, but not to harden their hearts. We want them to be wise, not cynical. It's a tall order—and we don't always get the balance right.

EXAMINING PERSPECTIVES ON FORGIVENESS

This is where forgiveness becomes essential, and yet so often misunderstood. As parents—and as people—we're constantly navigating that uncomfortable space between acknowledging wrong and holding open the possibility of redemption. From a Christian perspective, the idea that some people are just *bad* is not only mistaken—it's misleading.

No one is all good, just as no one is all bad, not even when they're very young. I find that most people agree with this in theory, but in practice, they often talk and behave as though the *nice* and *nasty* labels really do apply.

Psychologists call this the *fundamental attribution error*. It's the human habit of attributing our own bad behaviour to circumstances (I snapped because I was tired), but other people's bad behaviour to character (you snapped because you're a rude person).

Now, apply this to the playground. When *my* child lashes out, it's because he was provoked, or tired, or only five. When *your* child lashes out, it's because he's a troublemaker—or because *you're* not doing your job as a parent.

Christianity has more ancient language for this very modern problem—words like pride, lack of charity, concupiscence, and original sin. We may resist those terms, but both modern psychology and everyday experience point in the same direction: we're not as innocent as we'd like to believe, and others are not as guilty as we imagine.

What fascinates me is how this sits alongside the near-universal claim that people struggle with *low* self-esteem. We feel bad about ourselves, yet the evidence shows we consistently overestimate our own virtue compared to others. That's the fundamental attribution error again: I'm a decent person who sometimes messes up; you're just... less decent.

No child *ever* hurts another. That includes unintentional hurt, too. Working with parents on these friendship dilemmas has deepened my appreciation for something I used to barely notice: the Penitential Rite at the beginning of every Mass. It's where we confess together that we *have greatly sinned, in our thoughts and in our words, in what we have done, and in what we have failed to do.*

TEACHING CHILDREN THE ART OF FORGIVENESS

My colleague, a supremely qualified woman with degrees and diplomas in child development and counselling, had been unable to help her son move on. This was unusual, since she was a skilful parent, and her son was an easy-going boy. She had avoided the worst of the well-meaning parental approaches, like brushing it off, advising him to ignore the friend, or, even worse, suggesting some kind of retaliatory insult.

Then, one day, during an after-school playdate with another boy, a school-mum friend of hers had a chat with her son Ben (not his real name) about the situation, which she already knew about from previous conversations. This other mum listened, and then, in earshot of Ben's mother, she said, 'You know, it sounds like the kind of situation where the only solution is for you to forgive him.'

My friend was stunned by the suggestion. She mulled it over for the next few days before we met and told me the whole story. Having meditated on the fallout between the boys and the proposed solution of forgiveness, she had come to believe the ancient wisdom that there is emotional freedom in forgiveness.

She marvelled at how, despite all the tools at her disposal—from training in psychology, psychiatry, and child development—she had never been taught about the essential role of forgiveness in healing and moving beyond pain.

More than that, her son, incidentally, reacted well to the suggestion to forgive his friend. I find that children are often more able to forgive and let go of hurts than adults. It's as though the ability to forgive comes naturally to us, at least when it comes to forgiving those we love, like family and close friends.

FORGIVENESS AND PERSONAL FREEDOM

Over time, however, as hurt builds up, we seem to forget how to be as forgiving and cease to remember that we ought to be. Or maybe children gradually learn unforgiveness from the world around them, where resentment and revenge are far more prevalent than pardon.

The word *pardon* might sound stiff or formal, but in parenting, it's something we practise daily, often without realising. Some offences are easy to forgive; just about everything our infant children do to inconvenience or hurt us falls into this category. When children are little, forgiveness flows freely from your heart. You wouldn't dream of holding such tiny things against them.

Gradually, though, their offences become bigger and more painful. As your child grows, they start to feel as though they *should* know better, whether the injury is towards you, their other parent, a sibling, or a friend. Part of the problem is that these hurts are often hidden below the level of our proper awareness. By this, I mean that sometimes you're not even aware you're building up resentment towards your child.

Consider, for instance, how you feel when your six-year-old daughter deliberately hurts her three-year-old sister. Or when your ten-year-old son speaks to you in a contemptuous tone in front of other parents. Or when your seventeen-year-old son storms out of the house after screaming *You've ruined my life*, slamming the door behind him, leaving you to wonder if he'll come back at all. Are you in the habit of thinking of these as offences you need to forgive? If you're not, then there's a risk they're building up and getting in the way of your relationship with your child.

I was stunned when I started to realise just how many events require me to actively and consciously forgive, and how easily I held things against people. I was entirely familiar with the Christian ideal of *forgive us our trespasses as we forgive those who trespass against us.* I knew intellectually that I was meant to forgive over and over again, even the same person, for the same offence—but it turned out I hadn't been doing it.

I feel it's important to mention here that this is not an exhortation to forgive abuse by staying in an abusive situation. When I speak of forgiving the same offence by the same person over and over again, I mean situations where a child causes hurt due to immaturity or lack of skill, not cases of physical abuse or toxic relationships.

I believe the command to love others as we love ourselves compels us to leave such situations immediately. This does not contradict the call to forgive those who harm us. My experience with the kinds of harm that come even remotely close to abuse has taught me that it's much easier to forgive when you're out of harm's way.

I fail to see how it can be loving, for either the abused or the abuser, for an abusive situation to continue. Fear keeps people in abusive situations, not love. Love would leave.

FORGIVENESS IN ACTION

All my head knowledge about forgiveness was useless, however, as long as I wasn't taught how it worked in practice. I knew I *should* forgive; unfortunately, I didn't know *how* to forgive. This became a real problem when I had children.

Never having gained much experience of forgiveness beyond what came naturally, such as small hurts from people I loved, I was unprepared for how often this skill is required in life. At least, in my life, I would call it successful. And my definition of a successful life is one marked by lots of joy and peace.

Over the years, all the hurts and injuries I'd suffered added up until I became little more than a horrendous backlog of pain because I had no idea how to forgive and let go. I'd been raised on *Forget about it*, *Don't mention it*, and of course, *Sticks and stones may break my bones, but names can never hurt me*.

In other words, I learned how to minimise and deny my pain. But pain won't go away when it's handled like that. It might go underground, but it won't dissipate. It will slowly strangle your heart until your capacity to love is severely shrunken.

I know it's easier to blame our shortcomings, parental or otherwise, on others. And sometimes, it is appropriately compassionate to acknowledge how others' failings have contributed to our own. But deep down, if we pause long enough, we know there is much we could do differently to improve the quality of our relationships, regardless of how our struggles developed.

That's not to say we're capable of changing everything overnight. We may not be there yet. But the truth remains: there's much we *can* do if we're willing to learn. Fortunately for me and my family, learning to forgive was a challenge I was willing to take on.

WHY NICE ISN'T KIND

While I've learned to recognise all the little things that my son and daughter do (and don't do) that require ongoing forgiveness, I've also learned to acknowledge the ways I hurt them, and the forgiveness I need in return. Sometimes, I ask for it outright. More often, I simply admit the injury. And sometimes they say, "It's okay, Mum."

It sounds like minimising, but it isn't. I can hear the difference now. There's a softness in the tone of true forgiveness. Because to forgive is to love, and love is gentle. That tone is very different from the kind of *It's okay,* that is offered out of obligation or discomfort. That one sounds *nice* rather than *kind.*

There's a fear in saying *Actually, it's not okay—I'm still furious and not ready to let it go*. That's uncomfortable to admit, especially as a parent. When I've said something like that to my children—and I have—I've been aware that it sounds childish and even a bit vindictive. That's because it *is* childish and vindictive not to let go of anger sooner.

But sometimes, it's the best I'm capable of in that moment. And in a strange way, being honest about that keeps me in touch with my own sinfulness—how far short I fall from God's standard of love. For readers more familiar with the language of recovery than religion, this is the same territory we cover when we talk about *character defects*, or when we ask ourselves *What would love do?* However, you frame it, the truth is sobering. Despite the popular lie, I am not capable of unconditionally loving my children (or my spouse). Any fly on the wall of my home for 48 hours could confirm that.

I once heard that *nice = fear + anger*, whereas *kind = love + strength*. I thought about it a lot, testing whether it was true. While I wouldn't say I'm always angry when I'm being nice, I've definitely been nice while feeling angry and scared. Specifically, I've been nice when I was angry but afraid to admit it. That's when kindness, rooted in strength and love, feels almost impossible.

Let me give a familiar example. Your child refuses to leave a playdate when asked. They delay, or outright refuse, and you feel your anger rise. But you're also nervous—afraid of causing a scene in front of other parents—so you respond with niceness. *Okay, five more minutes*, you say, while trying to keep your tone even. You may not even realise you're afraid, except for a vague sense of social pressure. That's the kind of *nice* that stems from fear and anger. And parents do plenty of it—I certainly have.

Now contrast that with kindness. Kindness would insist, lovingly and firmly, that it's time to leave. That takes strength, because your child might persist in their refusal and even escalate into a full meltdown. You may have to carry a kicking and screaming child out of the situation—not pleasant for anyone. But it's the loving course of action.

And if you hold that boundary with empathy—acknowledging their disappointment but not wavering—it won't take many repeat performances before they learn that you mean it when you say it's time to go.

You don't love a child by letting them dictate when a playdate ends—or by letting the threat of a tantrum control your behaviour. It's an act of love to call time and stick with it, knowing what your child needs next, whether that's food, rest, or simply a calm, consistent parent.

WHEN IS STRENGTH THE KINDEST THING?

Self-love has a bad reputation in Christian circles, but I still believe we need to be loving to ourselves. It is not loving to ourselves or, ultimately, our children to place ourselves in situations where we are being dictated to by our children.

Parents are meant to be in charge of their children. That may sound old-fashioned, but it's built into the design of family life—biologically, culturally, and, in my belief, spiritually. In the Ten Commandments, this idea is made explicit: *Honour your father and mother, that it might go well for you in the land of your fathers.*

Modern parents are suffering dreadfully from the loss of their authority. Reasserting parental authority in a loving way is, I would argue, an act of self-regard. Even self-love.

All this is a long-winded way of saying: when you say it's time to go and your child objects, the kindest thing may be to ignore their remonstrations and leave anyway. And if that means picking up your child and removing them under duress, so be it.

Do that, and you'll likely find you have less need to forgive your child afterwards for humiliating you in front of other parents. Once the dust has settled, you may even feel a quiet satisfaction that you behaved like an adult and took charge, rather than like a hostage to your child's demands, only to end up resentful later.

In psychological terms, giving in like this is called *submissive behaviour*. The result? You undermine your authority, increase your own sense of powerlessness, and end up more stressed and harassed than before. Yes, you may have avoided a fight in the moment, but you're creating a rod for your own back in the long run. This is not kind to anyone—avoid the trap.

This kind of kindness, which has love plus strength, is also what it takes to forgive our children when we need to. Forgiveness takes far more strength than being nice. It's much easier to smile and say *It's fine* while still seething inside, too scared to say otherwise.

But niceness, when driven by fear or anger, isn't really kindness at all. It's much tougher to be kind—to speak the truth gently, to acknowledge our ongoing struggle to love, and to hold the line even when it's uncomfortable.

I've taken refuge in the knowledge that when I tell my child I'm still fuming with them, I'm giving them something of value: honest feedback about how their behaviour affects others. This kind of feedback is essential if a child is to grow into a decent adult—someone capable of real relationships, not just with family, but with friends, partners, and colleagues.

Some people might call this *tough love*, and in a way, they'd be right. But I think we often misunderstand that phrase. We use it to justify being hard on others, treating them coldly or sharply in the name of love. But real tough love is tough on *us*. It asks us to rise above our fears, our anger, and our wish to avoid conflict or maintain control. It's hard to stay kind when we're tired, triggered, or humiliated. But that's where strength meets love. That's where kindness lives.

If we shield our children from the truth of how they affect us, we fail to prepare them for how they'll affect others who won't love them like we do. Family often absorbs more than others will tolerate. And if you've ever heard your child complain about a classmate who hasn't learned how they impact others—too rough, too boastful—you know how this plays out. Poor awareness leads to poor friendships, poor relationships, and stunted lives.

Or maybe you're in the painful place where it's your child who's struggling to make or keep friends. If so, I want to assure you: you can help. But not always in the way you might instinctively think. Sometimes, true kindness doesn't look like rescuing or fixing or smoothing things over. It looks like becoming the kind of parent your child needs in that moment—more grounded, more accepting, more patient, more emotionally available.

You won't get there just by knowing what to do. You'll need grace—the kind that helps you become capable of doing what love requires. Ask God, your higher power, or the universe to show you how to be kinder and more loving to your child. That help will come. And yes, I do mean kinder, not nicer.

Passing on Lessons

As I've said already, not many of us are raised in such a way that we get a lot of practice at what's necessary for real forgiveness, but some people are. I am in awe of parents who teach this lesson well.

Because it wasn't taught well to my parents, or to their parents before them, it wasn't taught well to me either. So, I've had to learn it first in order to pass it on—and that's been a struggle. But God has been seeing to it that I learned this lesson, and I'm deeply grateful. The more I've worked on forgiving others—and myself—the more natural it has become to pass it on. As a result, I had the chance to teach it to my kids while they were still children.

Some of my closest moments with my daughter have been conversations about her struggles with forgiveness and unforgiveness. I've had to seriously practise what I preach to avoid the common pitfalls facing any parent trying to teach a child how to let go of hurts and move on.

On the one hand, listening to her when she's hurting means letting her pain take precedence over my discomfort. It used to make me want to make the pain go away quickly. This emotional discomfort often drives parents to minimise or rush in with solutions.

On the other hand, I've found that once my daughter has shared her pain and had a little moan (or a big moan), and I've listened with compassion for some time, it's important to gently invite her to let it go and forgive.

There's a real art to this: bring up forgiveness too soon, and you're likely to induce further fury. Your child now has two injuries to deal with: the original offence *and* the sting of feeling that you haven't understood the pain it caused. But please make sure you introduce it eventually. You must, if your child is to grow up with a heart capable of reaching out with trust to others.

If we don't teach this lesson, our children risk growing into adults with shrivelled hearts—hearts that long for love but are too scared to be vulnerable enough to feel it. To feel love, we must allow the possibility of pain. Many of us make a decision, often unconsciously, not to allow that to happen. It's a great loss when we choose to barricade our hearts behind fortified defences.

When Pain and Forgiveness Meet

The balance between feeling the pain and letting it go is a tricky one to get right. It's hard enough for us as adults, and even harder to teach children. Like all parenting, you feel your way in the dark. You will make mistakes (for which you will need to be forgiven).

If you are faithful in teaching your children this lesson, you will receive their forgiveness because they will know how to do it.

Try as you might or long for it with all your heart, your children will not get through childhood unscathed. Life will hurt them. Friends will let them down. The world will bruise them in ways you cannot predict or prevent. And each time this happens, you will have a beautiful opportunity to teach them the virtue of bringing pardon where there is injury.

You will learn that some offences need to be felt for quite some time before forgiveness can even be considered—Christian parents, I'm talking to you! Because the hurt runs deep. And even if the decision to forgive comes quickly, the pain may linger, so the choice may need to be made again and again.

You are bound to get it wrong many times. You'll miss hurts because you're too busy or distracted, or because the thing that upset your child wouldn't have bothered you. You'll encourage your child to forgive too quickly. And sometimes too slowly.

The bottom line is this: we hurt others, and we are hurt by others. All the time. That's the nature of our fallen world.

But when we learn—and teach—how to bring the spirit of forgiveness where there is wrongdoing, then we participate in the coming of God's kingdom. Not only in some far-off future, but here and now, in the love we offer one another, one injury and one pardon at a time.

4

Where There Is Discord, Let Me Bring Harmony

I grew up in a large Irish family that was loud, fun, and full of love, but not always harmonious. My parents, aunts, and uncles were devoted to one another, yet that didn't stop them from falling out, sometimes over something significant, often over something trivial.

The fallout could be brief or stretch on for months, even years. What didn't come naturally to us was repair. There was no grand reconciliation, no heartfelt apologies, or open conversations about what had gone wrong. Instead, when relationships did resume, it was usually without ever acknowledging the rupture. Whatever had happened was simply brushed under the carpet.

I suspect this was, in part, a way of preserving family bonds—an instinctive avoidance of making matters worse. But the cost was that wounds often remained unhealed beneath the surface, and the same conflicts had a way of repeating themselves.

Rupture is inevitable in human relationships. We will hurt each other. But there is a world of difference between hurt and harm, and it is the harm we must work to avoid. Nowhere is this more crucial than in parenting.

Parents and children will have moments of rupture as a result of misunderstandings, impatience, or emotional disconnects. But if we can repair those breaks, if we can model making things right, we teach our children something invaluable: that conflict does not have to mean separation, that love can withstand discord, and that true harmony is not the absence of disagreement but the ability to mend what has been torn.

STEPPING IN TO STEP OUT

One of the greatest challenges of family life is learning how to manage discord without becoming consumed by it. Nowhere is this more evident than in the daily squabbles of young children, especially siblings. Any parent with more than one child knows the familiar cycle: an argument over a toy, a game, or even a seemingly trivial point of pride escalating rapidly into frustration and tears.

In those moments, the temptation is strong: step in, impose a solution, and restore peace. But in doing so, we risk something greater than momentary disharmony; we risk depriving children of the chance to learn how to navigate conflict for themselves.

When peace is imposed rather than modelled, children may learn to avoid conflict altogether or to rely on authority to resolve it rather than developing the skills to engage with disagreement constructively. In shielding them from discomfort, we may unintentionally leave them ill-equipped for the inevitable discord of adult relationships.

When my children were small, about three and five, I encountered a parenting approach that changed how I handled their disputes. It came from Adele Faber and Elaine Mazlish's book *How to Talk So Kids Will Listen and Listen So Kids Will Talk*, a widely respected guide to family communication.

One of their strategies, *Step In to Step Out*, offered a simple but powerful way to help children resolve conflicts without parents assuming the role of judge and jury. The idea was to step into a conflict with just enough authority to remove an obstacle and then step out again, leaving the children to find their own way to a resolution.

I remember the first time I tried it. My children had fallen into yet another dispute because my daughter, still developing her grasp of boundaries, had irritated her older brother, who retaliated in turn. I could hear their voices rising from the playroom, early warning signals of a squabble heading towards full-blown tears.

Instead of rushing in to mediate, I experimented with *Step In to Step Out*. I entered the room, calmly surveyed the scene, and said something like, "Hmm, I see one toy and two children. This is a tricky problem." Then, without assigning blame or taking sides, I simply lifted the disputed item and placed it on a shelf—visible but out of reach. "I'm sure you two can find a fair way to solve this." And with that, I turned and left.

To my astonishment, within moments, they began negotiating. Who would have it first? How long would each turn last? How would they ensure fairness? They worked it out together, without tears, without me acting as referee, and, most importantly, without the resentment that so often follows when parents impose a solution.

It was one of my first real insights into what I later came to understand as the balance between parental authority and a child's autonomy: stepping in just enough to create structure and prevent real harm but stepping out quickly enough to allow growth.

This approach became a foundation not only for my parenting but also for my work with families. I often shared the technique in my private practice, and from it, I developed what I call my Bronze Rule: *Do not do for others what they ought to do for themselves.*

This principle is often overlooked in modern parenting, where well-meaning mothers and fathers, keen to protect their children from distress, unwittingly create unhealthy dependencies. Over time, these small interventions add up, and we see their consequences in children who struggle to problem-solve, manage frustration, or take responsibility for their own interactions.

Increasingly, educators, employers, and university lecturers observe that children and young adults lack the resilience and independence that previous generations seemed to develop more naturally.

In part, this stems from a shift in parenting—one driven by love but also by an unrealistic fear of conflict. Yet conflict, when handled well, is not harmful. It is formative. It teaches negotiation, compromise, emotional regulation, and, ultimately, the ability to live harmoniously with others.

Reflecting on all this, I couldn't help but compare it to my own childhood. In my large Irish family, disputes were common, but they were rarely approached with structured resolution. Arguments flared, loyalties shifted, and, more often than not, conflicts remained unresolved, simmering beneath the surface, or breaking out again in a different form.

The idea that conflict could be an opportunity—a chance to teach and learn harmony—was something I had to discover for myself and something I was determined to pass on to my own children because it is a skill truly worth learning—and one worth teaching.

RUPTURE AND REPAIR

The previous story was one of *avoiding* rupture, of stepping in early to prevent a conflict from escalating. But not all discord can be nipped in the bud. Sometimes, emotions flare, words or actions wound, and real harm is caused. When that happens, it isn't enough to let time pass and assume wounds will heal on their own.

One such moment of rupture happened when my children were a little older, perhaps six and eight. They had both been given Rubik's cubes, and my son, always methodical, was diligently learning to solve his. My daughter, on the other hand, had developed a rather creative approach: she would take a solved cube, twist a few sections, then twist them back and triumphantly declare that she had solved it. This infuriated her older brother, whose precise, logical mind could not abide what he saw as a blatant falsehood.

We were on holiday when this particular clash took place. Nia once again performed her little trick, proudly displaying her 'solved' cube, but this time, her brother had had enough. He snatched it from her, scrambled it completely, and handed it back with a cutting challenge: “See if you can solve it now.” His frustration had boiled over into deliberate cruelty, and its impact was immediate. Nia burst into sobs—deep, wounded tears, not just from the loss of her neatly arranged cube but from the unmistakable intent behind his actions. He had wanted to hurt her, and she knew it.

My husband and I looked at each other, recognising that this was one of those moments. It was no longer about a puzzle or a childhood squabble. A real injustice had taken place, and if we let it pass unaddressed, it would linger beneath the surface, unspoken but felt—a fracture in their relationship, the kind that, left unchecked, can accumulate over time. So, we did what we believed was necessary: we imposed not just a consequence but a path to repair.

Once we were home, we devised a plan. First, my son would have to give his Rubik’s cube to his sister, replacing the one he had effectively taken from her. More than that, he would have to use five euros of his own holiday money to buy her a small gift of her choosing. That evening, we took them both to a souvenir shop after dinner, where he—reluctantly but obediently—selected and paid for a small item she picked out.

Some parents might have felt this was too harsh, but we had seen too many examples, both in our own lives and in the lives of others, of resentment that festered when no meaningful repair was made. Siblings forgive each other over and over again—until, one day, *they don't*. The accumulated weight of small injustices, never acknowledged, can harden into something more lasting. When conflict is allowed to pass without repair, childhood grievances can stretch into adulthood, shaping sibling relationships for years to come.

Flynn was momentarily hurt by our intervention—his frustration flared, and his pride was wounded. But our concern wasn't about sparing him from discomfort; it was about shaping his character and guiding him away from something far more damaging. *A momentary hurt is not the same as harm.*

Allowing him to continue unchecked would have been risking something deeper: the hardening of a habit, a growing insensitivity to his sister's feelings, and the slow erosion of the kindness and integrity we wanted to nurture in him.

By the time my children reached their teenage years, something had become clear: the work of guiding them through these moments of rupture had paid off. They had become genuinely close, so much so that, at their senior school, they were known for being siblings who were also great friends. I was surprised to learn that this was not the norm. It seemed that many siblings had grown apart by the time they reached their teens, no longer seeing each other as allies but as rivals from a shared childhood.

Parents often believe they are neutral in sibling conflicts, but children perceive things differently. Studies show that many children feel their parents favour one sibling over another, even if no favouritism is intended.[1]

The failure to address injustice, whether real or perceived, leaves its mark. Harmony in a family does not mean the absence of conflict; it means having the tools to resolve it. And sometimes, resolution requires more than words; it requires an act of restoration.

LEARNING TO SPEAK

One of the hardest truths I have had to accept is that you cannot teach what you do not know. When my children were young, I learned—often by trial and error—how to help them navigate discord in a way that preserved their relationship and built their resilience.

However, there were lessons I had not yet learned myself: lessons about speaking up, expressing disappointment, and about facing conflict directly rather than avoiding it. And because I had not yet learned these things, I could not teach them.

I see now, particularly in my daughter, where my own gaps in understanding became hers. Nia, like so many girls, found the later years of junior school particularly challenging.

That delicate age from around nine to twelve is often an intense time for friendships among girls, with shifting alliances, unspoken tensions, and social dynamics that can be difficult to navigate. When she struggled to stand up for herself, to articulate her needs clearly, to say when something wasn't okay, I see now that she was mirroring something I had not yet learned to do myself.

At the time, I didn't have the skills to guide her through those moments. I could offer comfort, but not the tools she needed to advocate calmly for herself. But as I grew slowly, through my own learning, I was able to pass it on.

By her later school years and into university, she had begun to develop a quiet confidence, an ability to hold her ground and express herself in a way that I had once struggled to do. It was deeply affirming to witness—proof, perhaps, that even the lessons we learn late can still be of use.

This has been part of my own spiritual journey: learning to forgive myself for what I did not know, for what I could not give at the time. Parenting is humbling in that way since it lays bare our limitations, not just in knowledge but in emotional and spiritual growth. And yet, it also offers us a path forward. Because we are not fixed in place, and neither are our children.

This journey has not been limited to parenting. Even after twenty years of marriage, my husband and I discovered through outside help that we, too, had developed a pattern of avoiding conflict rather than addressing it. We both saw ourselves as open and communicative people, but in truth, we had been sidestepping certain difficult conversations for years, allowing small resentments to accumulate where honesty should have been.

For me, the greatest challenge was admitting disappointment. Having grown up in a family where conflict was poorly managed, I learned early on that difficult emotions—anger, hurt, disappointment—were best swallowed rather than spoken.

There was little space for expressing them in a way that felt safe, and so I became what many would call resilient. Strong, independent, unbothered. But this was not true resilience. It was simply avoidance. And avoidance, over time, breeds its own kind of discord.

When I felt disappointed in my husband, when he failed to notice something that mattered to me, or when I felt let down in some way, I found it nearly impossible to express it without blame. I would hold it in, minimising it to myself, trying to repress it, until eventually, it came spilling out in frustration or criticism. Needless to say, this did not foster harmony. It only deepened the divide, making it harder for us to truly understand one another.

In the past few years, I have had to learn a new way to lean into the discomfort of expressing my feelings honestly but without blame, to say *I was disappointed when this happened*, rather than letting my frustration speak for me. This small shift has had an enormous impact.

It has changed not only the way we handle conflict but the very atmosphere of our marriage. The silence that once held unspoken feelings has been replaced with something far richer: the kind of harmony that is not the absence of discord but the result of working through it together so something stronger can be built.

THE BALANCE BETWEEN TRUTH AND PEACE

Throughout this chapter, we've explored how harmony is not the absence of discord nor the mere suppression of difficult truths. It is something deeper, a way of engaging with conflict that seeks resolution without destruction, that honours both honesty and kindness. It is an onerous balance that demands both courage and restraint.

Growing up, I saw how discord festered when left unaddressed, how tensions lingered beneath the surface of my family's love. In recovery, I learned the wisdom of stepping back before reacting and choosing kindness over self-righteousness. At the same time, I have also seen how these same principles, when misunderstood, can lead to avoidance—an insistence on keeping the peace at any cost, even when real wounds go untended.

Christianity, 12-step recovery, and many spiritual traditions uphold patience and gentleness as virtues. *Just for today, I will not show anyone that my feelings are hurt.* There is wisdom in that. But if taken to an extreme, where we suppress every hurt, if we never speak the truth for fear of causing ripples, then what we call harmony is merely a fragile silence, not peace.

Proverbs reminds us that *a soft answer turns away wrath, but a harsh word stirs up anger* (Proverbs 15:1). This is the middle path. It is not about biting back every word indefinitely, nor is it about speaking every truth with reckless force. It is about choosing our words with care, knowing when to be silent and when to speak. It is about ensuring that our honesty is never wielded as a weapon but is always offered as a bridge to understanding.

In families, in friendships, in recovery, and in faith, real peace is found not in the absence of conflict but in how we move through it. The work of a peacemaker is not to avoid hard conversations but to enter them with love. Not to bury all wounds but to heal them with truth, spoken in gentleness and strength.

If we are to be channels of peace, we must commit not only to kindness but to integrity, not only to restraint but to courage. Not only to silence but to the right words, spoken in the right way, at the right time, so that true harmony may take root.

5

Where There Is Error, Let Me Bring Truth

The greatest error I ever made was believing I was not lovable. That was my dirty secret, my great shame. A part of me was convinced that if you truly knew me, if you could see inside my mind, you would realise how unlovable I really was. Another part of me clung to the hope that I was a reasonably decent human being, but I still feared that people didn't like me and never would.

I won't bore you with the long details of how these ideas took root, but suffice it to say that a mix of actual and perceived rejection throughout my childhood led me to a seemingly logical conclusion: there must be something profoundly wrong with me.

No one ever exposed this error. Without the opportunity for correction, the belief in my unworthiness grew unchecked. It thrived in the shameful darkness of secrecy, slowly strangling parts of me that were essential for thriving, especially my heart.

Reclaiming my self-worth has been a long and arduous journey. It has taken years to integrate the story of my childhood, to face the truth about my part in it, and to assign others their rightful share of responsibility. For a long time, I refused to see my own role and instead cast blame on others.

In a strange way, acknowledging the harm done to me was an act of confidence in an unconfident self. It felt validating to recognise that the wounds I carried were real, and the consequences of that harm were profound and long-lasting. Still, I regret how long I lingered in that space of blame, of myself and others. It is one of my deepest sorrows, and I have cried out to God for the harm I caused during those years when blame clouded my vision.

REVELATION OF TRUTH

God eventually showed me my great error, and I will be eternally grateful that he brought truth into the darkness of that deep lie. I have told the story of how I came to believe God loved me before, so I won't repeat it here. I will say again, however, that it is profoundly healing to realise you are loved by God.

How could I be unlovable when the omnipotent, omniscient, omnipresent, omnibenevolent God of the universe was telling me he loved me? And more than that, he had loved me with an everlasting love. To this day, I often remind myself of the beautiful truth that God has drawn me to himself with his everlasting love (adapted from Jeremiah 31:3). It is extraordinary to think that I passed through my entire childhood without internalising this truth. Somehow, despite being exposed to the idea of God's love for me, it did not penetrate my mind, heart, or soul. Instead, I ended up believing the opposite.

I know I am not the first and will not be the last human being to have believed she was unlovable. It is perhaps the most damaging yet widespread lie on the planet. It's no coincidence that the Bible is overflowing with reminders of God's unending, unconditional love for us. He knows we need this truth. It is a balm for our injured souls, a salve for our wounded minds, and solace for our broken hearts. It is the medicine that heals our greatest error.

Jesus came to heal the broken-hearted (Luke 4:18), and thank goodness he did because we, the broken-hearted, are everywhere. He has been busy for all eternity correcting the destructive errors lodged in our hearts. The error of thinking we do not need God. The error of assuming *we* can be God. The error is that God does not exist.

Today, some people labour under the error that evil does not exist—that there are only wrong choices, poor choices, or the best choices you could manage at the time. Somehow, we have managed to convince ourselves of this comforting fiction.

THE TRUTH ABOUT HUMAN GOODNESS AND SIN

Just as God revealed to me the truth of his love, he continually calls us all to face deeper truths—truths about ourselves, our sin, and the nature of good and evil. Thomas Merton, a notable spiritual author and Trappist monk, once wrestled with Buddhism before concluding that only Christianity fully addressed the problem of suffering and evil. Christianity is honest about our dual nature: we are made in the image of God, capable of great goodness, but also deeply flawed, capable of real sin. This truth, though obvious, is one we often resist.

Many today prefer to soften the language around sin, framing wrongdoing as mere error, poor choices, or unfortunate circumstances. We acknowledge the suffering others cause, but hesitate to name the harm we inflict on ourselves. Few people admit to being judgemental, or prideful, or gossipy—yet we all see these flaws in others. The very fact that we notice wrongdoing in the world should remind us that moral law exists. If we can recognise injustice, we must accept that justice is real. And if justice is real, then truth must be real, too.

Yet the truth is uncomfortable, and we prefer to keep it at arm's length. We want to see ourselves as good without confronting the moments when we are not. We hope for peace in the world while refusing to mend fractured relationships in our own lives. We wish for a just society while excusing the small injustices we participate in daily.

Christianity insists on both human dignity and human sinfulness. Without acknowledging our capacity for wrongdoing, we can't take responsibility for it. And without responsibility, there is no real transformation—only blame.

SUFFERING, FREE WILL AND THE MYSTERY OF GOD'S JUSTICE

One of the greatest errors that turns people away from faith is the problem of suffering. How could an all-good, all-powerful God allow a tsunami that kills 230,000 people in a moment? Why does he permit wars, childhood illness, or the cruel randomness of tragedy? It is natural to question God's goodness, or his existence, the face of such things. And yet, for me, the existence of suffering was one of the reasons I came to believe in God at all.

In the Bible, the Book of Genesis shows us that love requires freedom, but freedom makes evil and wrongdoing possible. If God forced goodness upon us, it would not be love. Any parent understands this instinctively: we long for our children to choose what is right, but we cannot *force* virtue without stripping them of their humanity. God, as the perfect Father, allows us the dignity of choice, both for good and for ill.

Yet suffering is not always the result of our own choices. Again, from the Bible, the story of Job teaches us that pain is not necessarily punishment. His suffering was neither deserved nor easily explained. This is where Christianity diverges sharply from the karma-based worldview I once found appealing. The idea that all suffering is the direct result of past sins—whether in this life or a previous one—may seem fair on the surface, but it leads to a cruel fatalism. A child born with a disability, a family devastated by war—under karma, these are not tragedies but consequences. Such a framework, rather than offering comfort, only deepens suffering by adding the burden of guilt. It is also, I came to see, a deeply unmerciful view of the world.

Christianity, in contrast, offers both justice and mercy. We are responsible for the wrong we do, yet we are not doomed by it. And we are not always the cause of our own suffering. This is why Christianity shaped compassionate societies—why hospitals, charities, and care for the suffering emerged and flourished in cultures steeped in its teachings. It acknowledges that suffering is real, but it also insists that suffering is not the end of the story. It is an error to assume that suffering is either meaningless or wholly deserved. Christianity offers the corrective truth: suffering is neither random nor necessarily a punishment, but it can be redemptive.

This is not only a more humane understanding of suffering but one that aligns with what we know about human psychology. A belief system that tells us we are always to blame for our pain fosters guilt and despair. Christianity, however, offers something radically different: the possibility of redemption, of meaning in suffering, and of love that endures beyond our failures.

Even beyond theology, modern psychology increasingly affirms what Christian teaching has long proclaimed—that human beings *need* grace. Studies on self-compassion show that those who approach their failings with mercy rather than harsh judgment are more likely to grow and change.[2] The same is true of forgiveness: those who forgive experience greater emotional well-being than those who cling to resentment.[3] In other words, the Christian model of justice tempered with mercy is not only spiritually true—it is psychologically healing.

I have come to believe that Christianity's vision of the human person is the truest one. It accounts for both our longing for justice and our desperate need for mercy. It affirms our dignity while acknowledging our frailty. And it insists, even in the face of suffering, that love is always the final word.

TURNING AWAY FROM GOD'S WILL

The Christian view of suffering also challenges us to confront an uncomfortable reality: suffering and evil often stem from our own resistance to God's will. We turn away from the truth that we are happiest when we live as God desires. We resist the idea that we are blessed when we honour our parents, show mercy to our enemies, rest, and worship God one day in seven, and uphold integrity by not committing adultery and reserving sex for marriage. These truths seem restrictive, inconvenient, and out of step with our desire to live as we please.

Instead, we buy into the lie that if it *feels* good, it must *be* good. We tell ourselves that if our heart desires something, it couldn't possibly be wrong. Yet, life shows us over and over that this is not true. The consequences of living outside God's will—broken relationships, inner turmoil, and a lack of peace—should guide us back to him, but often we persist in our rebellion.

THE SIMPLICITY OF GOD'S WILL

Rather than recognising that God's will brings us peace, we often complicate it. I used to believe that doing God's will meant doing something extraordinary, like going to Africa to work in an orphanage. If I weren't doing something visibly big, was I even living out my faith? Compared to other spiritual or religious people, especially certain Christians, I wondered if I was getting it all wrong.

This uncertainty gnawed at me. What did God want me to do? I was scared I was missing something. Was I not listening properly? Was I not hearing him? I would sit in church and look at the pastor's wife, who seemed to be changing the world with her ministry and wonder why my life looked so… ordinary. She was doing such good work and truly making a difference. By comparison, my own life felt unimpressive.

I read books like *Love Does* by Bob Goff and *Preemptive Love* by Jeremy Courtney, stories of people radically transforming lives in Uganda and Iraq. Meanwhile, I was doing school runs and making sure no one in my house ran out of clean socks. Was I missing some divine memo?

Then, one day, I stumbled upon the idea that God's will for me is always simple and always possible—today. Right now. This changed everything. I couldn't move my family to Uganda *today*, so that *couldn't* be God's will for today. Sounds obvious, but this realisation lifted a huge weight off my shoulders.

Of course, I *could* start the visa process and begin making arrangements—but that immediately violated the principle of simplicity. It would be an agonising, years-long ordeal. And that told me something: God's will isn't about striving or chasing impossible expectations. It's about showing up faithfully in the life I already have.

Finally, I took the *move to Africa* option off the table. God planted me here, and here is where he wants me to thrive. I don't need to manufacture some grand adventure—I need to live fully in the one I'm already in.

Besides, I hate camping, dislike travelling, abhor packing, revile living out of a suitcase, loathe logistics, and I have a strong aversion to being really hot (unless, of course, I can just lie around sleeping and reading). Clearly, I am *not* the one God is sending far from home. Someone else can handle the lifesaving, heatstroke-inducing heroics in Uganda. Phew.

This lesson—that God calls us to serve where we are—was just one of many truths he revealed to me as I grew in faith. Another equally transformative truth was about what happens after this life.

BETWEEN HEAVEN AND HELL

The more I kept walking with God, the more he kept bringing truth where there had been egregious errors. And he made it clear that I was meant to share some of what I was learning. Thankfully, I loved doing that. My husband and children became my captive audience—over dinner, breakfast, car journeys, and frankly, any time they couldn't escape. And as I shared, something happened—my husband followed me all the way back into the Church. I just couldn't *not* talk about what I was discovering (or rediscovering, really).

One of those discoveries was purgatory.* I was told about it as a child, and, of course, I accepted its reality. In fact, I worried a bit about getting stuck there if no one remembered to pray for me after I died. I absolutely assumed it would be my destination. Then, as I got older, I rejected this along with the rest of my faith. When I returned to God via various forms of Protestant Christianity, I wondered about purgatory now and then, but not enough to investigate. And then, finally, I looked into it.

God is perfectly holy, and only what is perfectly holy can come into his presence. Ergo, heaven can only be full of perfectly holy people. But at the same time, hell—eternal separation from God—must exist because love requires freedom. Yet hell is not what God wants for us, nor is it what most of us deserve.

How do you reconcile all of this?

You do it *through purgatory.*

---

* In Catholic teaching, purgatory is understood as a state of purification after death for souls who die in God's grace but are not yet fully sanctified. It is not a second chance at salvation but a process of being made ready for heaven, aided by the prayers of the living.

Purgatory is not just theologically sound—it is *logically necessary.*

When people hear Christians deny this third possible destination after death, they often recoil at the idea that eternity is a simple binary: saved or damned. The notion that salvation depends not only on having a specific religion or spirituality but also on adhering to a particular flavour of Christianity—whether that means undergoing full-immersion adult baptism (Baptists) or making a verbal declaration of faith (Pentecostals)—rightly offends our sense of logic. Surely, there must be a middle ground—an answer that acknowledges both God's mercy and his justice.

When I later encountered all the scripture verses in support of purgatory, they were just the icing on the cake. Logic had already led me there. Even C S Lewis, despite remaining an Anglican, accepted purgatory because it made too much sense to ignore.*

---

* While purgatory is a Catholic doctrine, the Eastern Orthodox Church also holds that the souls of the departed can benefit from the prayers of the living, though it does not define purgatory as a place of temporal punishment. Most Protestant traditions reject purgatory outright, but some Anglican and Lutheran theologians, including C.S. Lewis, have expressed belief in a form of post-death purification.

A RABBI'S OBJECTION TO GRACE

Once I saw the necessity of purgatory, I began to see how essential it was for reconciling both God's mercy and his justice. A while ago, I came across an anecdote in which a Rabbi shared a story that illustrated a major problem he had with Christianity. He recounted how he had once asked a Catholic priest to confirm if he had understood Catholic teaching correctly.

"Is it true," he asked, "that a Nazi who had worked in a concentration camp, sending Jews to their deaths, could profess faith in Jesus on his deathbed and be saved?"

The priest apparently answered, "That's the mystery of the grace of God."

The Rabbi was clearly disgusted. How could anyone believe something so illogical, so unjust?

But I think the priest in the story missed a crucial opportunity. Catholics do not believe there are only two destinations at the moment of death. We also have purgatory. A fuller Catholic response to the Rabbi would be this: yes, the Nazi can accept Christ on his deathbed and be saved, but he will almost certainly not gain immediate admittance to heaven. He will have to atone for every unrepentant sin in the purifying fires of purgatory.

Catholicism preserves God's perfect justice with purgatory. It also preserves his perfect mercy with the promise of salvation for all who choose it, no matter how late in life. It is logical, beautiful, and I believe, true.

The Relativism of Modern Truth

Purgatory demonstrates how truth must account for both justice and mercy. But what happens when the truth itself is denied?

Not so long ago, the ideas of *your truth* and *my truth* weren't mainstream concepts. But unquestionably, the idea that truth might not exist is an old one. After all, during Jesus' trial, when he claimed to have come into the world to testify to the truth, Pilate scoffed *What is truth?* (John 18:37-38).

Today, however, relativism has reached the point where it's difficult to have certain types of conversation at all. We have simultaneously elevated opinions to the status of truth while denying that truth can exist in the first place. It's an impressive contradiction—irrational, certainly, but humans have an extraordinary capacity for believing whatever suits us, rational or not.

Leaving aside the inconvenience this causes when you're trying to have an intelligent discussion, relativism has done real damage to the average family. It's one thing for French intellectuals to dabble in postmodernist thought experiments—*There's no such thing as truth* (is that true, I wonder?)—but it's quite another for a parent to face a defiant child without a grounding in basic, time-tested truths.

Like, for example, *honour your father and mother*. Or the simple idea that parents are supposed to be in charge of their homes. Or that a lack of discipline will spoil a child's character. We could debate all day about what effective discipline looks like, but the fact that discipline itself is essential should not be up for discussion.

And yet, in much of the Western world, it is.

Vast swathes of children are growing up without ever having been properly disciplined. As a result, they are left at the mercy of their instincts, their impulses, and their out-of-control emotions. And in turn, society is at the mercy of those undisciplined children.

This age of relativism has ushered in great uncertainty among adults, particularly parents, whose authority seems to be crumbling. And I am convinced that this loss of parental authority is contributing to the mental health crisis among children. If even the grown-ups aren't sure where the boundaries are, how can a child ever feel truly safe?

THE COST OF NEGLECTING CHILDREN'S NEEDS

This crisis of truth doesn't remain abstract. It seeps into the way we live and, most tragically, into the way we raise our children. A few years ago, a pupil at a senior school near my house committed suicide. Another student at the same school took their life last year. Rates of self-harm continue to rise. Eating disorders are increasing. Depression and anxiety among teens—and even younger children—are soaring. And these numbers only reflect those who meet clinical thresholds. They do not account for the vast number of children living with lower-level but still life-diminishing distress.

Let me tell you a story that illustrates the erosion of truth, parental authority, and the consequences of failing to meet children's fundamental needs. There are children across the UK who have been out of school for months or even years, trapped in bureaucratic limbo while waiting for suitable school placements. Some have ADHD, some struggle with anxiety, and others have complex social and emotional needs. Their families, often well-intentioned, find themselves in battles with the educational system, seeking the perfect solution, the right diagnosis, the ideal placement, while their children's lives drift by.

Take one such boy, thirteen years old, whose difficulties with attention and impulse control made mainstream school a challenge. He resisted attending, ran away repeatedly, and eventually, his parents stopped insisting. They agreed he could stay home permanently.

In past generations, this would have been understood as a discipline issue requiring firm parental intervention. Today, it is reframed as a mental health issue and a special educational need. The struggle to attend school is viewed less as a behaviour requiring correction and more as a symptom requiring accommodation. And so, the adults give in.

This child, like so many others, has multiple parental figures involved in his life. With more parents than average, one might assume he would receive an abundance of support. Yet, paradoxically, the opposite is often true. In complex family structures where responsibility is diffuse, decision-making can become paralysed. Each adult assumes someone else will step in. Each believes they are doing their best. But in the end, no one is taking full responsibility.

Instead of making hard choices—driving him to a school that meets his needs, enforcing structure, or holding firm boundaries—they spend their energy fighting the local authority, demanding that the government solve the problem for them. Their careers, commitments, and personal priorities take precedence, and so the system, rather than the parents, becomes the de facto guardian of the child's future.

The details of this story vary from case to case, but the underlying truth remains the same: when parents relinquish their authority by allowing institutions to bear the weight of their children's formation, children suffer.

The crisis goes beyond individual families. The erosion of parental responsibility is not just a personal failing but a cultural shift. We are living in a time when institutions—schools, the state, and mental health services—are expected to fill the gaps left by absent or disengaged parents. But no institution can replace what is meant to be given in the home: stability, discipline, and love that is both tender and firm.

Catholic teaching is unequivocal on this point. Children have a fundamental right to be raised in a family built on self-donating love. Pope St. John Paul II's *Theology of the Body* explains that the family is the first and most essential environment for learning love, trust, and identity. If parents will not take responsibility for their children's well-being, who will?

This is not just a religious belief. It is backed by modern psychology. Attachment theory and developmental research consistently show that children need strong, present, and attuned caregivers to develop emotional security. A child who lacks consistent, loving parental guidance often struggles with emotional regulation, impulse control, and long-term resilience.

Even international law agrees. The UN Declaration on the Rights of the Child states that children have the right to be raised by their biological parents whenever possible. The logic is simple: children need adults who will show up for them. And yet, in progressive circles, where rights are often championed, this right is strangely overlooked.

When children's fundamental needs are ignored, the consequences are severe. First, many are denied the right to be conceived within a stable family. Then, some are denied the right to be raised by their biological parents. Finally, they are denied the parental leadership they so desperately need.

That is not ideology. That is reality.

THE TRUTH BEYOND FEELINGS

One day, I saw a child wearing a T-shirt that read: *Feelings come, feelings go.* It struck me as a surprisingly deep message—one that both children and adults often forget. Modern parenting, much like modern culture, has absorbed the idea that feelings are the highest authority. If a child is upset, then something must be wrong. If they are angry, they must have been wronged. If they are sad, then something must be fixed. But feelings come, and feelings go. And they are not always a reliable guide to truth.

This misunderstanding is at the heart of many parenting struggles today. Parents, wanting to be kind, often mistake their child's momentary discomfort for a deeper injustice. They assume that if their child is sad or distressed, they must change course—give in, soothe, adjust, and stop whatever is causing the upset.

But discipline, by its nature, involves discomfort. Learning restraint involves frustration. Accepting limits can be painful. And yet, these things are necessary. If we only ever parent according to what makes a child happy in the moment, we will fail to parent in a way that makes our children strong, secure, and wise in the long term.

Just as purgatory is the necessary purification before entering heaven, childhood itself is a formative process—a series of necessary discomforts and small purifications that shape a child into a well-formed adult. No parent relishes seeing their child in distress, but there are moments when the right thing to do is to let them feel it and grow through it.

A young child denied the toy they desperately want at the shop will feel angry. An older child who is required to put down a screen and greet a guest will feel momentarily aggrieved at being corrected. A teenager who is told they must revise for an exam instead of going to a party will feel frustrated. However, none of these feelings mean the parent is in error. Truth does not change just because a child—or an adult—finds it inconvenient or difficult to bear.

The modern world teaches us that emotions define reality, but emotions are fleeting. Christianity, on the other hand, teaches that truth defines reality and that truth is often demanding. A good parent, like a good teacher, a good mentor, and a good God, does not shield their child from every moment of struggle, frustration, or grief. They walk with them through it, helping them grow into someone who can bear difficulty with grace and wisdom.

The truth remains true, even when it is painful.

Feelings come; feelings go.

But the truth remains.

6

Where There Is Doubt, Let Me Bring Faith

Doubt is a universal human experience. It gnaws at us, whether it's about our ability to succeed, whether we are lovable, or whether we are worthy. As a behavioural psychologist, I've spent years observing how deeply self-doubt can shape lives. It stops people from applying for jobs they'd excel in, from forming relationships they'd thrive in, and from pursuing dreams they were made for. The struggle with self-worth is real, and it's one of the most insidious ways doubt takes root.

It's easy to think that in today's world, where self-esteem is old news, we'd have solved this problem. And yet, anxiety and depression continue to rise, particularly among young people. Despite decades of effort to nurture confidence in children, we seem to be missing the mark. If self-esteem could be raised by sheer encouragement, then the generations raised on *You can do anything!* and *You're special just as you are!* should be thriving. Yet, we see more self-doubt than ever. What went wrong?

Faith in oneself is not about believing you are flawless; it is about believing you can face challenges, survive setbacks, and keep moving forward. It is a kind of trust that says *I can handle this*. True confidence is not a feeling—it is a belief grounded in experience, in the knowledge that you have met challenges before and can do so again. It is, in essence, a type of faith. And like all faith, it is something that must be cultivated.

12-STEP INSIGHT: SELF-ESTEEM COMES FROM DOING ESTEEMABLE THINGS

One of the great truths I've learned through 12-step recovery is that self-esteem does not come from being told you are wonderful—it comes from doing estimable things. Confidence is not built in a vacuum; it is the natural result of achievement, however small. When a three-year-old learns to do up their own zip, when a five-year-old crosses the road without holding a parent's hand, when a ten-year-old does the ironing, when a fourteen-year-old takes the train alone for the first time, each of these moments builds competence. And competence is the foundation of true self-esteem.

As parents, we are often tempted to wait until we are fully comfortable before allowing our children to take risks. But if we wait until *we* feel completely ready, we will likely wait too long.

The boundaries of challenge must be elastic—sometimes expanding beyond our comfort zone, yet within reason. The discernment challenge is real: what one ten-year-old is ready for, another twelve-year-old may not be. Parenting requires both reason and intuition, coupled with real awareness and knowledge of your child. We must balance the necessity of pushing our children forward with the wisdom of knowing when to say no.

THE COMPETENCE TRADE-OFF: HELPING TOO MUCH HURTS

Dr Daniel Amen, a renowned psychiatrist and neuroscientist, describes this dynamic well: if you do too much for your child, you boost your own self-esteem at the expense of theirs. It is a sobering thought. So much of what we do as parents is done out of love, but sometimes our love turns into overprotection. The goal should not be to eliminate all struggles from a child's life, but to equip them with the skills to handle them.

Psychologist Erik Erikson identified key stages of development, and one of the most critical is the stage of *industry vs. inferiority* (approximately ages 6-11). If a child successfully navigates this stage, they develop a strong sense of competence. If they do not, they internalise self-doubt and feelings of inferiority that can follow them into adulthood.

Faith in oneself is ultimately about competence—the belief that you have the ability to meet the challenges of life. And competence, unlike the self-esteem movement's hollow affirmations, is built on experience. This is why overprotecting children backfires: it removes opportunities for them to prove to themselves that they can handle things. The more we do for them, the less they believe they can do for themselves.

THE INEVITABLE TRADE-OFF BETWEEN PHYSICAL AND PSYCHOLOGICAL SAFETY

Over the years in my private practice, I have heard many versions of this dilemma from parents. What follows is a composite story drawn from their experiences. A young boy has been cycling safely in the front garden, but now he's starting to venture beyond the gates without permission. His mother is terrified of the dangers outside—the roads, the unknown risks. She asks me how she should handle it. Should she punish him? Administer some sort of consequence? Set stricter boundaries?

At first, she thinks he is simply being defiant. He knows he's not allowed outside the gate, yet he does it anyway. She feels frustrated, wondering why he won't listen. But as we discuss it, she quickly begins to see the situation differently. He isn't defying her for the sake of defiance—he is responding to an innate drive to expand his competence. His development is pushing him forward, compelling him to take on new challenges.

Once she understands this, her frustration melts into recognition. She sees that her role isn't to suppress this drive but to facilitate it in a way that balances safety with growth. I've observed that a lot of defiance in children can be understood as them railing against boundaries that are too tight. When a child feels capable of more than they are allowed to do, they will push against the rules, not because they are inherently rebellious, but because they are striving for mastery over their world.

A child who never learns to navigate real-world challenges—be it cycling on a quiet road, managing money, or handling social interactions—will grow into an adult who is unprepared for life. There is an often unacknowledged trade-off between a child's physical safety and their psychological development. Parenting requires frequent discernment, knowing when to let go and when to hold firm.

When you take this approach—letting your children stretch themselves—they will inevitably fall on occasion, and some of those falls may be scary. They miss their train stop, and you have to rescue them; the cycling challenge proves too tough, and they end up in the hospital; the party they were sure they were ready for had alcohol, and they got drunk without meaning to. This is part of the learning process. Often, the natural consequence is enough, and as a parent, you don't need to do anything more. Or perhaps you need to take more time to teach what has not been learned yet. Or you might need to review the boundary and tighten it again, saying no to the next party or mountain bike challenge.

Building Responsibility Through Experience

I think of how we approached teaching our teenage son about the importance of timekeeping as he increasingly began to venture out on his own. He found it hard at first to be home on time. We used an array of consequences, both natural and imposed. We discussed our desire to know, within reason, where he was and to be free of worry when he was out late. We explained how, if something had gone wrong, we needed to know whether to call the police or not, and that time was of the essence in these situations. In other words, we were open about our needs as parents while not ignoring his needs for independence and autonomy. By the way, for a teenager, having to listen to a parent lecture on parental needs is a kind of consequence!

We also gave him the benefit of the doubt—he's quite the daydreaming type, so we trusted that we were only dealing with forgetting, not defiance—and reminded ourselves to be patient as he learned this new lesson. We leaned on each other to manage our discomfort when he was late and not to pester or micro-manage him. But we also used penalties and sanctions. When you're trying to teach independence and consideration for others, taking away opportunities to practice isn't an ideal sanction. So, we used financial penalties—e.g., if you're late, you will have to pay a fine—to help you remember! People remember events that have emotional salience, so linking lateness with a financial penalty was highly memorable for our son, who is more financially motivated than our daughter, and helped him learn to be on time more quickly.

There were moments when we wondered whether our approach was too harsh (or too lenient!), just as he might have doubted whether he would ever remember to keep track of time or whether his parents were being fair. But doubt is a natural part of any learning process, whether it's about something as small as timekeeping or as profound as faith itself. We cannot grow in confidence without first wrestling with uncertainty.

Bringing faith where there is doubt means showing children (and reminding ourselves) that our setbacks are not failures, that our struggle is not a sign of weakness, and that we are stronger than we believe. It means stepping away from coddling and moving towards encouragement, giving support without removing the challenge. It is an act of love to let our children wrestle with difficulty, knowing that through it, they will grow stronger.

Wrestling with Belief

Faith in God is often framed as something you either have or don't have, like a talent for singing or an ability to parallel park without holding your breath. But for most of us, faith is something we struggle with, perhaps pick up and put down, lose and rediscover.

I grew up in a house where faith was… well, let's say, fluid. My father, a man of great integrity and a strong sense of right and wrong, has never been one for religious observance. He attends the necessary rites of passage—baptisms, weddings, and funerals—but otherwise stays in his seat, silent and still, as if he's an impartial observer rather than a participant. I have no idea what he really believes deep down, and I suspect he'd struggle to articulate it himself. But one thing I do know is that he's not indifferent. He has an opinion on God, the Catholic Church, and religion in general. It's negative. Over the years, I've noticed that many people who claim they don't believe in God still manage to be quite angry with him.

My mother, on the other hand, is a Catholic of the *God and I are grand, but I'll not be dictated to* variety. She believes in God, enjoys the music at Mass, gives to the Church (despite my father's grumbling about it), and considers herself Catholic. But she picks and chooses. She believes in God's love but isn't terribly concerned with the finer points of doctrine. She has her own list of religious rights and wrongs, and she holds to them with the conviction of a Pope—but a Pope who doesn't believe in purgatory, isn't sure about hell and thinks annulments are just Catholic divorces with extra paperwork.

With a foundation like that, it was hardly inevitable that I'd end up a practising Catholic. In fact, my faith dwindled in early adulthood, leaving me functionally agnostic for years. Then, in my darkest moment, I found myself drawn back to the idea of God—not as a distant deity but as a source of hope, of meaning, of something greater than myself. My journey back to Christianity took years, each step marked by deep scepticism, reluctant acceptance, and eventual conviction.

School, Mrs O'Connor and the Mass Test

Of course, I had plenty of religious instruction at school. I was educated by nuns and lay teachers who took their faith seriously. Some of them were kind, some were fierce, and some were downright terrifying in the way only small Irish women armed with Bibles and sharp glances can be.

Mrs O'Connor was one of those teachers who, I think, genuinely cared about our spiritual formation. Every Monday morning, she would conduct a Mass quiz to make sure we'd been paying attention the day before. Not just "Did you go?" but "What were the readings about? What did Father say in the homily?" This led to an underground economy of Mass leaflets being shared among those who hadn't gone, so they could try to bluff their way through.

Looking back, I can see that Mrs O'Connor probably thought she was instilling reverence, commitment, and the importance of engaging with our faith. I suspect her methods did not achieve quite what she hoped. What she actually taught me was an ability to think on my feet and a deep-seated fear of being asked questions I'm not prepared for. It was a strange form of catechesis—half devotion, half survival training.

Arguably, the most important thing Mrs O'Connor taught me, though, which has been invaluable in my role as a parent, is the idea that you've got to keep your eye on what your children are really learning rather than what you're hoping to teach.

LOSING AND FINDING FAITH

Given all of this, I suppose it's not surprising that I walked away from the Church. The faith of my childhood vanished overnight in my first year at university, and I barely noticed it was gone. Partly, I was simply too busy to think about it—lectures, parties, and an exciting new social life were far more interesting than bothering with the many rituals and rules of Roman Catholicism. But, looking back, I can also see there was a deeper reason. The way I wanted to live—sex and drugs and rock and roll, in the grand old tradition—clashed entirely with the moral structure I'd been raised with. And since I didn't particularly want to change my behaviour, the simplest solution was to jettison the belief system that was causing the problem.

For years, I wasn't so much an atheist as a committed dabbler in alternative spiritualities. Faith didn't disappear altogether—it just shape-shifted into something more palatable to the life I was living. I drifted between various strands of New Age spirituality and Eastern philosophies, eventually settling on a vague kind of à la carte Buddhism crossed with Wiccan Paganism. I had no particular loyalty to any of them, just a general sense that some kind of higher power might exist, provided it didn't ask too much of me.

But there is something about faith that refuses to let you go entirely. It lingers at the edges of things, waiting for a moment to step back in. For me, that moment came in my mid-thirties when life took a turn for the worse, and I decided to seek recovery. When everything felt too heavy, when I had exhausted all my own resources, I found myself drawn back—not out of blind belief, but out of something deeper, something more instinctive.

Gradually, all the beliefs I had abandoned as a teenager—the idea that there really was a higher power, that life had a purpose beyond my own immediate wants, that perhaps I was not the centre of the universe—began to creep back in. Not because I was looking for them, but because I could no longer ignore them.

My faith returned, not all at once, but piece by piece. At first, I simply acknowledged that something bigger than me existed. Then, over time, I had to admit that if God existed, he was not just an abstract force but a presence with meaning. Eventually, I accepted that the God I had known as a child, one I had walked away from, had been patiently waiting for me all along.

Passing on Faith Without Force

When I became a mother, I thought a lot about how faith is passed on. It is natural to long for our children to embrace the things that have brought us new life. Yet this desire must be balanced with the reality that faith is deeply personal; it cannot be forced or rushed.

One of the trickiest situations arises when the adults in a household disagree on how to practise faith within the family. My husband and I found ourselves at odds about how frequently to attend Mass with the children. His instinct was to bring them every Sunday without fail, while I took a more flexible approach, aware that attempting to force faith could easily backfire. Navigating this tension required effort at open dialogue, respect for each other's perspectives, and an understanding that if one person experiences a spiritual awakening, it does not guarantee others are in the same place. Ultimately, we resolved this family challenge in our own deeply imperfect, messy way: sometimes, I supported his desire, and sometimes he accepted mine. Our children responded in line with their individual differences in temperament. Our cooperative son came to Mass more often than his little (re)sister.

Of course, part of why we wish to pass on our faith is that we believe it offers tremendous protective benefits. It gives children a sense of belonging and moral grounding, and it connects them to a loving and supportive community. Yet we must also remember that no matter how precious and true it feels to us, faith remains a personal choice. In many recovery programmes, there is an idea that resonates strongly with this reality: *attraction, not promotion*. When children see our faith drawing us towards empathy, love, and peace, they are more inclined to be curious. If we lapse into heavy-handed methods or attempt to steer them by fear or obligation, their hearts can withdraw.

For Christians, there is a further example: Jesus was attractive. People followed him in large numbers, though a few were scandalised or outright appalled by his teachings. Still, the crowds came because of the authority and profound love he radiated. I am fond of saying that if the way we are practising our Christian faith is not attractive to people, then we are doing something wrong. When we embody patience, humility, and kindness, we remove obstacles that might block our children from experiencing the essence of what we believe.

And so, we circle back to *where there is doubt; let me bring faith*. In practice, this means meeting our children's questions—and our own struggles—with calm assurance rather than dogmatic insistence. If they hesitate or push back, we have an opportunity to live our faith in a way that gently reassures them. The best ambassadors for the reality of faith are parents who live it wholeheartedly. When children witness the healing, growth, and transformation that flow from a genuine relationship with the divine, they are naturally drawn to explore it for themselves. In that open space, faith becomes something they choose rather than something we impose, and in that choice lies the seed of a faith that can withstand storms.

DOUBT AND FAITH IN THE CULTURE

Doubt doesn't just affect individuals—it seeps into the culture we live in. In fact, in recent years, doubt has been elevated to a virtue, while faith, at least traditional religious faith, has been increasingly treated as something quaint at best and dangerous at worst.

For centuries, belief in God was a given. People might have questioned aspects of doctrine, wrestled with personal struggles, or fallen short of their ideals, but the existence of a higher power wasn't generally up for debate. Now, we live in a time when certainty itself is seen as suspect. The only thing we seem sure of is that we can't be sure of anything. Doubt is fashionable. Scepticism is clever. Faith? Well, faith is naïve.

It's an odd reversal. We congratulate ourselves on having thrown off the shackles of rigid belief, only to become rigidly dogmatic in our rejection of it. The new orthodoxy is one of constant questioning, but only in the approved direction. Certain beliefs—traditional views on marriage, family, and biological sex—are now considered not just outdated but unacceptable. The old heretics were those who doubted religion; the new heretics are those who still hold to it.

I've watched this shift with fascination. It has been particularly stark in the case of tolerance. I grew up being told that tolerance was about allowing for different views, even ones I disagreed with.

That's not what tolerance means today. Now, tolerance demands not just acceptance but affirmation. Anything short of a full-throated endorsement is seen as bigotry.

Take the issue of gender. We have, in the space of a decade, gone from a culture that recognised the reality of biological sex to one where questioning the idea that *transwomen are women* is enough to get you labelled a transphobe. It is not enough to respect the dignity of every person or to extend kindness and compassion—you must also adopt the language, the ideology, and the worldview. And if you don't, you are cast out.

I find it particularly ironic that those who speak most about inclusion seem to have very little room for people like me, people who hold to traditional Christian views but do so with genuine love and goodwill. There is no curiosity about why we believe what we do, no attempt to engage. It is simply assumed that our views are rooted in ignorance or hatred.

THE SHIFT FROM DOUBT TO CERTAINTY

What fascinates me most is that, in the name of questioning, many people have become more rigid than the religious fundamentalists they claim to oppose. We hear a lot about how religion is dogmatic, but I have never seen a doctrine enforced as ruthlessly as the current cultural orthodoxy.

There is no room for nuance. If you do not affirm, you are denying the existence of. If you do not celebrate, you are condemning. Doubt—once seen as a healthy part of intellectual and spiritual development—is no longer tolerated when it challenges the accepted norms.

It reminds me of something G K Chesterton, the English writer and philosopher, once said: "The purpose of an open mind, like an open mouth, is to close on something solid." But modern culture seems to have misunderstood the point. We keep our minds so open that we refuse to let them settle on anything. Certainty of any kind is seen as dangerous except, of course, for certainty about *that*.

WHERE DOES THAT LEAVE FAITH?

So, where does all this leave people like me—people who are not looking to impose our beliefs on others but who also do not want to be forced to abandon them?

I come back, as I often do, to the Catholic Church. For all its flaws, it is one of the last institutions that still stands firmly for truth, even when that truth is unpopular. It does not bend to cultural trends. It does not rewrite its doctrines every time a new ideology takes hold. It is today as deeply unfashionable as it has ever been.

And yet, that is precisely why I trust it. If the Church had been making things up as it went along for two thousand years, it would have collapsed centuries ago. The fact that it has endured—not because of human cleverness, but despite human failings—tells me that something more than human is at work.

Faith, real faith, is not just about personal belief. It is about being anchored to something solid in a world that is increasingly adrift. It is about having the courage to stand by the truth, even when that truth is unpopular.

I think of a mother I know whose preteen daughter confided one evening that she thought she might be gay. The mother, instead of reacting with alarm or rushing to affirm something that may not have even been true, simply took it in stride. She told her daughter that she loved her and that there was no rush to figure anything out—that many girls her age weren't interested in boys yet and that not being drawn to them at this stage didn't necessarily mean anything at all. She reassured her that girl-crushes on cool older girls and favourite teachers have always been part of growing up and that she didn't need to put herself into any box just yet.

The next morning, her daughter came to her and said, "Um, that thing I said last night—can we just forget about that?"

Some might argue that this mother should have taken a different approach, that she failed to affirm her daughter's first tentative attempt to come out. But the reality is lots of preteens are not yet sexualised and are simply trying to make sense of themselves in a hyper-sexualised world. This mother chose to sow faith where there was doubt, to offer a steady presence in the midst of cultural confusion. And crucially, if she ever needed to revisit the conversation, she could. One parenting moment does not make or break a relationship. It is a *pattern* of not listening, not caring, and not engaging that damages trust over time.

Of course, some might claim her retraction the next morning was evidence that she'd been shamed into silence—but there's no such trace in the story. Just a child who felt safe enough to wonder aloud, and safe enough to change her mind. And if she ever returns to that conversation, her mother will be ready, steady, listening, and unafraid.

Bringing faith where there is doubt does not mean refusing to question. It means being willing to hold to the truth even when everything around us is shifting. It means having the humility to acknowledge that we do not create reality—we discover it. And it means remembering, always, that truth and love are not in opposition. Faith that is real, like love that is real, is not brittle. It does not shatter under pressure. It endures.

And perhaps, in a culture that worships relativism, the most radical thing we can do is to stand firm in faith, not as a weapon, but as an anchor.

7

Where There Is Despair, Let Me Bring Hope

It is so very easy to fall into despair about our children. You might not call it despair, but I would bet you've felt it or something close to it. Every parent needs to learn to recognise this feeling, not just because it is common, but because it is entirely destructive.

Sometimes, what we call worry—a gnawing sense that something might go wrong—is simply fear in a more socially acceptable disguise. Other times, what starts as self-pity—the quiet resentment of how hard parenting feels—can deepen into something darker if left unchecked. Despair rarely arrives all at once. More often, it creeps in through the back door, starting as fear, anxiety, or even sheer overwhelm, growing into a sense of hopelessness if we fail to challenge it.

For some parents, despair manifests as the secret conviction that there's something fundamentally wrong with their child, making the relationship feel impossibly difficult. For others, it's the overwhelming urge to quit—to step back and let their children figure things out alone because it all just feels too hard. It might appear as persistent anxiety that your child won't turn out alright, or as self-blame, the nagging belief that you are failing as a parent. Sometimes, it takes the form of endless complaining, voicing our frustration instead of facing our deeper fears.

However, despair manifests in you, it's crucial to recognise it for what it is and to root it out before it takes hold. Left unchecked, it will not only make *you* miserable but also make you miserable to be around. It can poison the atmosphere in your home, making your children more prone to despair. Over time, it can even create a self-fulfilling prophecy, entrenching negative patterns in your parenting and your child's development. In such a toxic emotional environment, your children won't thrive as they ought to.

Worst of all, despair is a lie.

HOPE AND PRAYER: THE ULTIMATE WEAPONS

Even in the most desperate of situations, there is no need to give in to despair. It might feel inevitable, but it is not. The truth is: despair is never the only option—there is always reason to hope.

At the end of the worst day, when you've sunk into hopelessness without realising it, you can still haul yourself out of that gloomy place by choosing to bring hope. What could there be to hope for at the end of a desperate day, you might think? Well, you could hope that tomorrow will be better. You could hope that your children will forgive you when you make amends for being in such a negative mood all day. You could even hope for something as simple as the willingness to start over again in the morning.

As Christians, or simply as people seeking renewal through faith, if we have anything at all, we must surely have hope. Yet it seems we often focus on certain aspects of our faith while overlooking others. The Bible makes it very clear that Christians are meant to be hopeful. *May the God of hope fill you with all joy and peace as you trust in him, so that you may overflow with hope by the power of the Holy Spirit* (Romans 15:13).

THE SEDUCTION OF WORRY AND THE PULL OF DESPAIR

And yet, many Christians today spend much of their time worrying—about the state of the world, the people in charge, the refugee crisis, the wars in Ukraine and Gaza, the shortage of priests, the corruption in the Church, the environmental crisis, the abortion crisis, the youth of today. The list could go on endlessly.

This kind of worry feels seductive. It seems like the right thing to do, as if a concerned member of the human race ought to be tormented, at least a little, by these terrible realities. But my answer is an emphatic no. If we worry like this, we are disobeying God.

Of course, we are all sinners, and that means we disobey God regularly. But the goal of being Christian is to grow into sanctity, which means striving to align our lives with God's will, even in the small, seemingly insignificant things. In recovery terms, we might call this continuing to make spiritual progress, practising spiritual principles in all areas of life, not just the obvious ones.

For me, this includes trying to obey the Bible's most frequent command: *Be not afraid.* If we allow worry and fear to dominate, we risk ignoring God's will for us. In recovery, we are given a similar spiritual directive: to continue watching for selfishness, dishonesty, resentment, and fear. When these crop up, we ask God at once to remove them. Am I saying we should never feel afraid, worried, or even despairing? Not at all. God gave us emotions, and the gospels make it clear that Jesus himself felt the full range of human emotion.

The struggle is not in avoiding fear or despair entirely but in refusing to cultivate it. For consummate worriers, I recommend reading Jesus' *Lilies of the Field* passage from the *Sermon on the Mount* (Matthew 6:25–34). Read it once. Then, read it again. And again.

While the St. Francis prayer talks about bringing hope to places of despair, most people don't immediately think of bringing hope into the places of despair in their own lives. As people in recovery, we may be so focused on making amends and being of service that we forget to offer ourselves the same grace. As Christians, we often focus on what we can do for others who are suffering, overlooking the importance of tending to our own pain.

And, of course, I'm not saying you shouldn't bring hope to a friend who is in despair. But you can also seek hope for yourself, not only in prayer but by reaching out to someone who can listen and remind you of the truth when you've lost sight of it. We sometimes resist doing this, telling ourselves we should be strong enough, or that our faith should be enough, or that after all these years in recovery, we ought to be able to handle it alone. But these are lies.

Hope is not usually something we find alone. While it can be reached in solitude, history offers examples of extraordinary individuals who have kept hope alive even in isolation—it is more often discovered in connection. In recovery, this is why sponsorship exists: to offer guidance, encouragement, and the simple reassurance that we are not alone. Hope often arrives through the kindness and wisdom of another person, through the simple grace of being heard.

If this resonates, consider whether you tend to conceal your struggles. Maybe no one but you realises you're suffering from despair about your children. Perhaps you hide your difficulties at home out of shame, only letting yourself feel despair late at night when the house is quiet. Maybe then you cry and give in to overwhelm and the bleak thoughts that are the hallmark of despair.

So, how do you bring hope where there is despair? Isn't it ludicrous to believe that when you're feeling despair, you can suddenly feel hope instead? For sure, if despair is a habit for you, it's not going to disappear overnight. But it can start to improve overnight. I entirely recommend that after you read this section, you start to pay attention to your moods and be on the lookout for despair.

SURRENDERING WORRY, FINDING HOPE

Before I could even begin to recognise despair, I first had to surrender my tendency to worry, learning to entrust my children to God rather than living in near-constant fear for them. God began taking my worry from me, lightening the burden I had carried for so long. At the time, I thought that was the whole lesson. I didn't yet realise that worry was just one layer of something deeper. The full extent of that realisation would only come later.

In order for me to properly understand the impact of despair in my life, God laid the groundwork with two significant spiritual experiences that brought a massive reduction in my worry about my children, particularly my daughter, who, out of my two children, is the one I am more inclined to worry about.

The first of these experiences planted the seed of hope, leading me to return again and again to a verse from Jeremiah (29:11): *For I know the plans I have for you, says the Lord, plans to prosper you and not to harm you, to give you hope and a future.*

God spoke these words into my heart shortly after rescuing me from the worst of my destructive compulsions. Meditating on them had been a balm to my bruised and battered spirit. They soothed my fear, took away my dread, and began to heal my broken heart. God had plans to prosper me. He had a wonderful plan for my future.

But I still worried like crazy about my daughter. On occasion, I was more than worried—I cried out to God, challenging his decision to make her the way he did.

"What were you thinking?" I would cry. "How on earth could you have thought it was a good idea to make her so stubborn? So defiant? Why are her emotions *so big*? And why, oh why, will she not sit still?"

At the time, I thought the best that could be said about my prayers was that they were heartfelt. But the more I kept honestly connecting with God and taking *all of me* to prayer—the frustration, the fear, the exasperation—the more I came to see that this was actually part of a deeply biblical tradition. The Psalms are a marvellous read for anyone struggling with negative emotions, particularly despair. They show us that God doesn't demand polished prayers; he invites honesty. My mistake wasn't in crying out to him—it was in failing to move beyond my cries to a place of trust and hope.

One day, while on holiday at my parents' place in Spain, I picked up a daily meditation book by Sr Stanislaus Kennedy. As I flipped through it, I came across a page featuring the words from Jeremiah 29:11. For reasons I don't entirely understand, reading them that morning pierced me in a way they never had before.

Suddenly, I knew—deep in my soul—that these words weren't just a promise from God to me; they applied to my daughter, too. She was God's daughter as much as mine. No matter how much I loved her, God loved her even more. He would draw her to him, just as he had done for me.

The realisation brought me a profound sense of relief and peace, followed by grief that I hadn't believed sooner. I saw clearly that every moment I had spent worrying about her wasn't just wasted but harmful. I repented deeply and cried out to God for forgiveness, which, of course, he had already bestowed.

PRACTICE, PRACTICE, PRACTICE

From that day on, I began the long journey of learning to trust God more with my children. But it wasn't easy. Patterns of worry and self-pity were deeply ingrained, and trust—deep trust—was something I had to grow into. The lessons I was learning didn't transform me completely overnight. Like peeling an onion, I found that each new stage of growth revealed deeper layers beneath. Just when I thought I had moved past such negativity, I would encounter it again in a new form, requiring me to revisit old lessons with fresh understanding.

I found myself returning to these same lessons when I took up the habit of praying the St. Francis prayer weekly and meditating on it between times. At first, I thought I was simply deepening my prayer practice—but of course, it revealed something uncomfortable. By now, I had spent years acknowledging emotions like worry, self-pity, and feeling overwhelmed, but I still hadn't recognised despair for what it truly was. I had softened it with more modern, palatable terms, framing it as catastrophising or reacting instead of responding. Dismissing it as frustration, exhaustion, or even dysregulation. These prevented me from seeing the stark reality. But the St. Francis prayer didn't let me hide. It forced me to name despair as despair, and that naming was what finally allowed me to break its hold.

It was humbling. Yet, with the prayer as my weekly reminder to bring hope where there was despair, I began to make real progress. I remembered the advice of a spiritual mentor who had told me to *practice, practice, practice* the opposites of my worst character defects. I saw clearly how unattractive despair was—not just in others but in myself. It was bleak, whiny, and often untrue. I knew it had to go.

But letting go of despair didn't just mean replacing it with hope—I also had to change how I related to myself in the process. One of the most important lessons I learned was that when I struggled, I didn't need to berate myself for failing. I needed to offer myself the same compassion I would offer to anyone else in pain.

I had struggled before to show compassion to parts of myself I didn't fully accept. Earlier in my recovery journey, it was my younger selves—shy little Janey and her defiant teenage counterpart—who tested my patience the most. But now, I was facing something even more challenging: extending that same grace to my present self.

In Nonviolent Communication (NVC), this is called *self-empathy,* which is learning to listen to yourself with kindness rather than judgement. It's a skill I didn't even realise I lacked. So often, when I felt discouraged, I would double down on self-criticism instead of pausing to acknowledge my struggles with gentleness. But I began to see that if I truly wanted to bring hope where there was despair, I had to start with myself.

This is why I call self-compassion the Silver Rule—*doing unto yourself what you would do unto others*. We all know the Golden Rule, but how often do we apply this principle in reverse? If we are speaking to ourselves in a way we wouldn't speak to a struggling friend, something is wrong. If we want to bring hope into the world, we have to stop poisoning our own well with harsh self-talk and despair.

With God's help, I became entirely willing to let go of despair. I asked him to take it from me and practised its opposite, hope. It's so helpful to know the virtue that opposes your favourite vice so you can actively cultivate it. For me, this meant choosing to hope again and again, even when despair felt more familiar. But it also meant choosing *kindness towards myself* rather than slipping into shame or self-pity. Or choosing kindness towards myself *when* I slipped into shame or self-pity.

And, like everything else, it took practice.

A LESSON IN HUMILITY

Does this mean I never fall into despair now? Not at all. After writing the last paragraph, I took a break to watch my daughter play netball. Her team lost badly. She seemed fine at first, but hours later, all her disappointment and frustration came pouring out.

By the time I'd listened, spoken (possibly too much), and exceeded my limit without realising, I found myself back in despair. I'd picked the wrong school, and my daughter was a disaster. That night, I decided again to let go of despair and remember hope.

The next morning, I went to Mass and heard a reading from the Book of Job: *When will this night end? He laments.* I laughed—it was a timely reminder to choose hope over despair. Once again, I marvelled at God's sense of humour and how he arranged the universe to teach me humility at just the right moment.

And so, I offer this chapter to anyone who has ever struggled with despair about their children. I've been there, and I'll likely be there again—but hopefully not too soon.

Years more have gone by since I first wrote down these lessons, yet one of the greatest gifts I can still give my (now adult) children is to entrust them to God daily, remembering that he exhorts me to hope. I hope that they will be alright. I have faith that he will make up for my failings, and I trust that he will keep them close to his heart. Above all, I hold fast to the promise that he has plans to prosper them and give them hope and a future. Knowing this, I have no need to despair.

8

Where There Is Darkness, Let Me Bring Light

I didn't come to understand a truth that changed everything in a single moment. Instead, it grew within me over time: the realisation that darkness, no matter how powerful it seems, holds no true power at all. This understanding brought with it an increasingly profound sense of peace and clarity. It is why good will ultimately triumph, because light is infinitely stronger than darkness. Even the deepest, most impenetrable blackness can be dispelled by the smallest glimmer of light. And even when all feels lost, it never truly is. This truth freed me from so much of the fear and anxiety I had carried. In the largest, darkest room, a single match—tiny, fragile—draws the eye and pushes back the shadows.

Once I understood this, I began to see its echoes everywhere. Depression, anxiety, shame, and addiction can feel like endless shadows, places where hope feels unreachable. The weight of poverty, crime, and cruelty may deepen the void. Anger, pain, or hatred may seem like reasonable responses, but they often make the darkness more suffocating. Yet no matter how heavy the shadows are, the power of light—of hope, love, or understanding—remains undeniable. Whether it's a tiny flicker or a blazing flame, light is always there, ready to illuminate the path forward.

Darkness, while daunting, is part of life's rhythm, but it does not have to define us. Light, however small, holds a power that far exceeds its size. Darkness isn't an equal opponent to light; it is simply the absence of it. The moment light appears, darkness begins to yield. Night follows day, just as Winter inevitably gives way to Spring. Over time, pain eases, fear diminishes, and hatred fades—because light always finds a way to return.

WHEN DARKNESS SPEAKS

There wasn't just one moment when darkness spoke to me, but this was one of the loudest. I was in my early twenties, lost in the haze of addiction. At the time, I told myself it was a lifestyle choice, a phase of youthful experimentation. The truth was far less glamorous. I was clinging to a toxic relationship with a boyfriend who was equally entangled in his own darkness.

That night, the darkness didn't just surround me—it spoke. I saw it in the form of a serpent, coiled and writhing on my boyfriend's right shoulder. It wasn't really there, of course, but if you've ever experienced a hallucination, you know how real it feels. The image unnerved me to my core. It was as if the shadows themselves had taken shape to deliver a message, a warning about the life I was living and the man I was with.

At first, I tried to rationalise it away. *It's just the drugs,* I told myself. *Party drugs do this to people.* But no matter how I tried to dismiss it, I couldn't shake the feeling that this serpent meant something.

I stared at it for hours, willing it to dissolve back into reality. I knew my boyfriend's shirt was plain red, yet I couldn't make the serpent disappear. It writhed and twisted, refusing to let me forget. It felt like a reflection of everything I was trying to ignore: the destructiveness of our relationship, the grip of addiction, the life I was refusing to change.

I wish I could tell you I listened to the warning that night, that its message jolted me awake and set me on a better path. But I wasn't ready. Instead, I clung to comforting excuses. The hallucination? Just a side effect of the drugs. The unsettling feeling in my chest? Something I could numb with another night of partying. I convinced myself to forget the serpent, but some part of me—perhaps the part of me still reaching for light—couldn't let it go entirely.

REFLECTION ON THE DARKNESS SPEAKING

Looking back, I now see the serpent as more than just a figment of my imagination. It was a symbol of the life I was living—a warning about the man I was with, the choices I was making, and the deeper truths I was unwilling to face. At the time, I dismissed it as nonsense, a hallucination born of my own subconscious. But in hindsight, I like to think it was the voice of light breaking through the darkness of my life, speaking a truth I wasn't yet ready to hear.

Living as I was—in the grip of addiction, anxiety, and unresolved pain—this voice of light felt deeply uncomfortable. It disturbed the fragile illusions I had built to survive, and its unsettling nature made it easy to dismiss. What I didn't understand then is that this is often how light speaks to us in times of darkness, not with comfort, but with unease, urging us to confront truths we'd rather avoid.

Years later, through Ignatian spirituality, I found a framework that made sense of this experience. The Ignatian method of discernment revealed a profound truth about the voices of light and darkness: when we are mired in shadows, the voice of light often unsettles us, while the voice of darkness soothes us, lulling us deeper into our pain. But when we step into the light, the roles reverse—God's voice brings peace, while the voice of darkness sows fear and anxiety.

In hindsight, I understand the serpent as a moment of grace, a spark of awareness planted in my heart. It was God speaking, calling me to wake up and see the life I needed to leave behind. Though I wasn't ready to act on it then—wasn't ready to leave my boyfriend or make sweeping changes—the experience set something in motion. That night, I decided to stop using hallucinogens. It wasn't much, but it was a start.

This moment marked the beginning of my journey back towards the light. Over time, that small flicker of awareness grew, guiding me through years of struggle and self-discovery. The serpent wasn't just a hallucination; it was a signpost pointing me towards the path I would one day walk. Just not yet.

A GLIMPSE INTO THE ABYSS

After the serpent incident, the darkness deepened. Each night brought a suffocating dread as though sleep might claim me forever. My body felt leaden as if bound by invisible chains. I fought to move—small, deliberate gestures—to convince myself the paralysis wasn't real. But the fear was overwhelming, and I couldn't shake the sense of an evil presence pressing in around me.

These nights were haunted by an indescribable malevolence, a shadowy force that seemed intent on seeping into my very being. I told no one, fearing that sharing this would lead to a diagnosis of madness, or worse, institutionalisation. Only much later did I learn this phenomenon had a name: sleep paralysis. Yet even knowing that, a part of me still believes I had touched something beyond the material, glimpsing a spiritual battle playing out beyond my understanding.

In the past, these experiences were called visitations by evil spirits. And though science offers explanations, I remain convinced that what I felt was a real, fleeting awareness of the struggle between darkness and light. When faced with such raw, primal evil, terror is inevitable, especially when you have no foundation of faith to anchor you, no trust in the triumph of the light.

Desperate for comfort, I sought solace in whatever rituals eased the fear. Placing a crystal on my forehead, basking in the sun's warmth, or listening to Irish artist Mary Black's *No Frontiers*—these became my lifelines. The song's lyrics, with their themes of hope and harmony, seemed like a fragile thread connecting me to something greater. They whispered of good prevailing over evil, of light piercing through the darkness. It felt like theology woven into melody, and I clung to it with everything I had.

Having abandoned the faith of my childhood, I was left adrift, vulnerable to nihilism and the void it brings. But somehow, through these small comforts, I began to rebuild. Slowly, the nightmares faded, the heaviness lifted, and life moved forward. Yet the memory of that darkness and the battle it revealed remains, a reminder of how easily we can lose our way without the guiding light of hope.

WITH FAITH COMES GREAT POWER

Fast forward a dozen years, and the darkness descended again. This time, though, I faced it with my faith in God firmly intact. The experience was transformed by this foundation. I no longer needed to cling solely to secular songs for comfort, no matter how beautiful they were. Yes, I revisited *No Frontiers*—its message still resonates—but now I had the Psalms, and especially Psalm 23, as my refuge:

The Lord is my shepherd; there is nothing I shall want. Fresh and green are the pastures where he gives me repose.

In 2008, we lost everything in the financial crash. I was newly sober, newly faithful, and deeply anxious. Yet, I did not let the circumstances consume me. As I learned to rest in the words of Psalm 23—*Near restful waters He leads me to revive my drooping spirit*—I began to understand the wisdom in not letting tomorrow's worries overwhelm today.

Jesus' *Lilies of the Field* teaching came alive for me during this time. *Do not worry about tomorrow, for tomorrow will worry about itself* (Matthew 6:34). The simplicity of trusting that God provides, just as he clothes the lilies and feeds the birds, became a balm for my anxious mind. It was a lesson I clung to: worrying about the future only robs the present of peace, and most fears never come to pass anyway.

Still, the battle wasn't easy. My thoughts churned endlessly, anxiety filling my mind like a washing machine stuck in a spin cycle. My head was a dangerous neighbourhood, and I knew better than to wander it alone. How does one escape their own thoughts?

I read a self-help title once: *Change Your Thoughts, Change Your Life.* While this idea aligns with New Age philosophy, it also has parallels in Christian theology. Jesus, too, emphasised the significance of our thoughts. He taught that the man who lusts after a woman in his heart has already committed adultery, and the one who harbours anger towards his brother has already sinned.

Though we are more than just our thoughts, they shape our lives and our connection to God. I began to see that with faith, I could challenge and redirect my thoughts. Trusting God meant trusting not only in his provision but also in his ability to transform my mind, bringing peace where there had been chaos.

THE POWER OF SELF-AFFIRMATION

I have long been comfortable with the principles behind Rhonda Byrne's *The Secret* and similar teachings. Like Oprah and other proponents of positive thinking, I believe our thoughts matter deeply. There's no conflict between this and Christianity in my view—both acknowledge the importance of managing our minds. But the question remains: how best to guide our thoughts?

For much of my life, especially the years I lived without an explicit belief in God, I relied on self-affirmation. It can be incredibly powerful. Positive self-talk propelled me through university, pushed me to conquer fears, and even helped me leave a damaging relationship to find my husband. I once crafted my own affirmation, inspired by Louise Hay's *You Can Heal Your Life*:

I have a loving, joyous relationship. A successful, rewarding career. And an exciting, intimate, fulfilling life.

I repeated it so often that I still know it by heart. It brought focus and confidence, but it never addressed the deeper issue:

shame. Self-affirmation, no matter how effective, couldn't fully reach the parts of me that needed healing. How could I fix myself when I was also the problem? It was a paradox I couldn't solve.

When faith returned to my life, I discovered a source of affirmation far greater than my own words. The Bible is filled with affirmations—verses that light up the darkness and anchor the soul. As I've mentioned, Psalm 23 in particular became a lifeline:

He guides me along the right path. He is true to His name.

Though I'd sung this psalm in childhood, its full meaning only came to me later. When the financial crash of 2008 left us facing severe insecurity, those words became a refuge. Without even realising it, I had begun praying through the Psalms. I wouldn't have called it praying then, but as I sang and recited the words, I felt peace replacing anxiety.

I also came to understand St. Paul's instruction to *take every thought captive* (2 Corinthians 10:5). It felt like discovering that Cognitive Behavioural Therapy had been hidden in the Bible all along. Whenever anxiety threatened to overwhelm me, I would catch the thought, redirect it, and replay my beloved Psalm like a broken record in my mind.

Slowly, the promises in those verses transformed me. The melody soothed me, but the words did more: they reshaped how I thought, anchoring me in hope. I began to rise each day not with a flood of self-criticism, but with a quiet assurance that God was leading me along the right path.

Affirming myself had carried me far, but faith carried me deeper. Where self-help ended, the Word of God began, dispelling the darkness and reviving my spirit in ways I never imagined possible.

THE IMPACT OF MATERNAL DEPRESSION

This psalm gently guided me out of the darkness and into the light—a transformation for which I am profoundly grateful. It taught me a truth I now hold close: you cannot bring light to someone in darkness if you are not walking in the light yourself. If we are to be conduits of God's light, we must first allow it to illuminate our own shadows.

Those of us who believe in Christ and the immense power of his love are called to reflect that light into the world. Nowhere is this more vital than in parenting. Research clearly shows that maternal depression can have devastating consequences for children, affecting their emotional resilience, cognitive development, and even physical growth.[4]

And yet, this is a truth we seem reluctant to confront. Beyond academic circles, the reality of maternal depression's impact on children is often dismissed, denied, or simply not discussed. That silence is costly, not just for mothers, but for their children. Depression is a treatable condition. While no single treatment works for everyone, and while much remains to be improved, there is hope. Facing this uncomfortable truth could pave the way for healing and transformation for families in need.

It is not that mothers with depression don't love their children—they often do deeply. But depression can cloud their ability to express that love in consistent and nurturing ways. The psychological literature describes this as *poor maternal responsiveness and attunement* or *intrusive interaction patterns*. At its heart, this means that a mother struggling with depression may find it difficult to offer the kind of outward-focused, self-giving love her child needs to thrive.

Depression, by its nature, turns the focus inward, while love requires reaching outward. A child raised by a mother ensnared by depression may grow up feeling unloved, not because love isn't present, but because it cannot fully manifest through the haze of despair. Recognising this is not about blame; it is about understanding the profound need for healing and support.

Transformation is possible, and there is great power in choosing hope, love, and faith over the darkness of despair. This is not meant to trivialise the immense struggle of depression—it is a heavy burden to bear—but to remind us that change begins with awareness and a willingness to seek help. Loving others, especially our children, often calls us to rise above ourselves. And while that may not be easy, it is a truth we can carry gently in our hearts: love and healing begin when we step out of the shadows.

THE IMPACT OF PERSONAL CHOICES

I do not exclude myself from the challenges and truths I explore here. In fact, it is through grappling with my own struggles that I've come to these conclusions. When I recognised the negative impact my drinking was having on my children, particularly my daughter, I made the decision to stop. At first, I didn't stop drinking for myself; I stopped for them. My love for my children, though obscured by my actions, ultimately motivated me to face the consequences of my behaviour honestly and make a change.

It's important to acknowledge, however, that not everyone is able to overcome something as complex as a drinking problem, even out of love for their children. Addiction, depression, and other challenges are powerful and multifaceted, and the journey towards healing can be long and difficult. For me, while the initial push came from wanting to protect my children, staying stopped required me to do it for myself. Only then could I sustain the transformation that also benefited my children.

I believe that compassion must be at the heart of any conversation about these topics. Christians are called to see the dignity in every person, created in the image and likeness of God, and to treat them with love. This includes those struggling with depression or addiction. Compassion, however, does not mean avoiding uncomfortable truths. True love sometimes requires facing the consequences of our actions and acknowledging the harm they may cause, even unintentionally.

Depression, for example, is often described as a state of hopelessness. While this may be an organic illness for some, it is also a spiritual struggle for others. Psychiatrist Glòria Durà-Vilà has written powerfully about the importance of distinguishing between clinical depression and what Catholic mystics have called the *dark night of the soul*. Thinking of depression in spiritual terms does not dismiss its seriousness or complexity; rather, it offers hope for healing through the transformation of thought and faith. It reminds us that even in the darkest valleys, there is light, and change is possible.

This is not to minimise the challenges faced by mothers at risk for depression, especially postpartum. Being a new mother can be isolating and overwhelming, even in the best of circumstances. When compounded by poverty, lack of support, or systemic inequality, as seen in the disproportionately high rates of postpartum depression among young, poor, and unmarried mothers, this burden becomes even heavier.[5]

I remember my own early struggles with motherhood vividly. Though I was blessed to have a supportive husband, I still found myself thinking *This is so tough! I used to have an interesting job and my own time, and now I'm home alone with a completely dependent baby. I'm bored, I'm lonely—help!* I cannot imagine how much harder this would have been if I had been doing it alone.

These experiences remind me that people and their struggles are complex. A child may feel both compassion for a struggling parent and anger over the consequences of that struggle. Both emotions are valid. While it is natural to avoid difficult conversations, avoiding the truth rarely leads to healing. Grappling with dark truths, however painful, can ultimately lead us into the light, transforming despair into hope and brokenness into love.

When we combine truth with compassion, we create space for transformation, not just for individuals but for entire families. This is where faith, love, and hope intersect, offering a path forward even in the midst of darkness.

UNDERSTANDING DEPRESSION WITHIN A SPIRITUAL CONTEXT

If you are a Christian suffering from depression, and the idea that it could be connected to disobedience feels upsetting, take heart. We all fall short of God's glory—every single one of us. As St. Paul reminds us in Romans 3:23: *All have sinned and fall short of the glory of God.* Depression is not a sign of being a worse sinner than anyone else, and my intention here is not to imply spiritual superiority simply because depression is not one of my heaviest crosses.

The truth is, I have wrestled with despair myself. While for me it might not rise to the level of clinical depression, the experience of hopelessness is the same in essence. Whether you call it despair, dysthymia, or depression, the difference is one of degree, not kind. And when I find myself stuck in those dark places, I've learned that staying there too long is dangerous—not only for me but for those I love. It separates me from God's light and the outward-focused love he calls me to embody.

But here's the beauty of faith: God does not leave us in the darkness. Depression may feel like a chasm too deep to climb out of, but God's love can reach the darkest recesses of our minds and hearts. *I have loved you with an everlasting love* (Jeremiah 31:3).

That love calls us out of darkness and into the light, no matter how far we've fallen.

Perhaps you're holding this book because you need that reminder. Not to feel judged but to feel hope. God is not finished with you. He sees your pain and your struggle, and he longs to draw you close. Repentance is not about guilt—it's about turning towards the light and trusting that his grace is greater than your despair.

The question is: Will you listen to his voice? Will you trust in his love, even when the weight of darkness feels unbearable? Faith doesn't erase the struggle, but it transforms it. It brings hope where there was none and a path where there seemed to be no way forward.

THE TRANSFORMATIVE NATURE OF REPENTANCE

Some years ago, I listened to Eckhart Tolle discuss repentance. For those unfamiliar with him, Tolle is a prominent New Age teacher who draws heavily from various spiritual traditions, including the teachings of Jesus, though he interprets them through his own lens. He described repentance as a mistranslation of the Greek word *metanoia,* arguing that it doesn't mean feeling sorrowful, as we often assume, but rather *turning around* or changing one's thinking.

While I agree that repentance involves a profound shift in perspective, I part ways with Tolle and others who suggest we should discard the idea of sorrow from the concept of repentance. In my experience, true repentance is both a change in thinking and a recognition of the harm caused by our past actions. Feeling sorrow for that harm is not only appropriate—it's transformative.

How else could I look back at my past behaviours and desire to move beyond them if I didn't first acknowledge the pain they caused? Sorrow is not an obstacle to repentance; it's evidence of this deeper understanding. When we feel genuine regret, we naturally want to change to ensure we don't repeat those mistakes. This is why sorrow and repentance are so intertwined.

As parents, we intuitively understand this. When our children apologise for misbehaving, we don't just want to hear the words *I'm sorry*. We look for signs of genuine regret—visible indications that they understand the impact of their actions. Sorrow is what transforms a mere apology into true contrition and creates the desire to avoid repeating the behaviour.

For me, repentance was a deeply emotional process. When I realised I had been living in darkness—hurting myself and others—it wasn't an intellectual exercise. I wept. The tears came not because I was told to feel sorrowful but because sorrow was my natural response to seeing the truth of my actions and their consequences.

That said, I recognise that not everyone expresses sorrow in the same way. Cultural and biological differences mean men, on average, cry less than women, but that doesn't diminish the depth or validity of their feelings. Jesus shows us the way here: he wept when it was right to weep. He didn't avoid tears, nor did he force them. Whether we cry or not, what matters is the sincerity of our contrition and the transformation of our hearts. No one cries the wrong way, or fails to repent if tears don't come.

But sorrow alone isn't enough. True repentance also involves turning around, changing the way we think, and committing to a new way of being. Repentance, then, is more than just regret for past harm; it's an active, forward-looking process. It's a recognition of the darkness, a decision to step into the light, and a commitment to walk a different path.

If the Christian tradition has historically overemphasised the sorrowful aspect of repentance, we now have the opportunity to restore its full meaning. Feeling sorrow for our sins is crucial, but it's only one part of the journey. Changing our thinking, embracing the Good News, and allowing God's love to transform us—that is the essence of repentance.

This book is, in many ways, an account of my own repentance: how I turned around, wept for the harm I caused, and came to believe in the hope and promise of the Gospel. Repentance is not an outdated, burdensome concept; it's a path to freedom, to light, and to love.

INTERWOVEN PATHS OF HEALING AND REPENTANCE

I used to wonder if it was possible to heal without tears. I believe that for some of us, it's not. Similarly, I've doubted whether true repentance is possible without any tears. By now, I've come to see repentance and healing as deeply interconnected—perhaps even the same thing. The extent to which you repent is often the extent to which you heal.

Of course, not everyone weeps in the same way—or at all. As I noted earlier, men and women differ in their tendency to cry, both for biological and cultural reasons. However, research shows that tears are not all the same. We don't just cry from emotion; we shed different types of tears—basal, reflex, and emotional—and these vary in their chemical composition.[6] Emotional tears, the kind most associated with sorrow and catharsis, contain stress hormones and other chemicals that seem to play a role in self-regulation.[7] In other words, we don't cry just to express our feelings; we cry to process them. Crying is part of how the body seeks equilibrium, just as sweating cools us or sleeping restores us.

This doesn't mean that those who cry less—or not at all—are definitely unrepentant or unhealed. We all regulate our emotions in different ways. Jesus wept when the moment called for it, but he did not weep at every moment of grief or sorrow. His example shows that what matters is not whether we express sorrow through tears every time, but whether we allow ourselves to be transformed by truth. Some find their release through weeping, others through stillness, prayer, or action. Nevertheless, I think there is something to the idea that repentance is needed from the very things for which we seek healing.

This may sound ridiculous or harsh, especially if you view depression or other struggles as burdens imposed upon you rather than something to repent of. But I think this way because I understand repentance as healing. Repentance is not about guilt or punishment; it's about turning away from the darkness and stepping into the light. It's a process of acknowledging harm, both to ourselves and others, and seeking restoration. You may disagree, but I encourage you to sit with the idea. You might find it more appealing—and more hopeful—than you expect.

One last word about how God draws us out of the darkness and into his light. Christians are meant to be marked by joy and great love. Jesus said, *By this, everyone will know that you are my disciples: if you love one another* (John 13:35). In recovery, we speak of becoming happy, joyous, and free. Whether we express it in the language of faith or recovery, the message is the same: a life lived in truth and healing should bear the fruit of love and freedom. If we find ourselves lacking this love, freedom, and joy, something is wrong.

Timothy Radcliffe, in his book *What is the Point of Being Christian?* suggests that the absence of joy may indicate that we are still living in fear. I think he's right. Fear is a rational response to the world's darkness—it is, after all, a scary place. The malevolence, suffering, and apparent meaninglessness of life can weigh heavily on even the most faithful hearts.

The thinkers of the Enlightenment and the new atheists didn't intend to rob people of meaning or condemn them to lives of quiet despair. But in the absence of faith, this is often the result. Even those of us who believe can find ourselves infected by this pervasive sense of futility.

Yet the Good News remains: *The people living in darkness have seen a great light* (Isaiah 9:2; Matthew 4:16). This light shines in the darkness, and the darkness cannot overcome it. It is always there, waiting for us to open our eyes and see.

For those of us who have glimpsed this light, the call is clear: we must carry it into the world. But we can only bring the light to others if we ourselves are filled with it. The Great Commission—*Go and make disciples of all nations* (Matthew 28:18)—begins in our own homes and hearts. The best way to live this mission is to become a saint in your family and let your life be a beacon of hope and love.

This is what it means to step out of the darkness and into the light. This is what it means to say *Where there is darkness, let me bring light.*

9

Where There Is Sadness, Let Me Bring Joy

Have you ever seen a child drop an ice cream? It's a small tragedy played out in slow motion—the cone slips, the scoop wobbles, and then—splat. For a moment, there's silence as the child processes what just happened. Then the face freezes, and the corners of the mouth quiver. And finally, the heartbreak arrives—a face crumpling, a wail piercing the air, and tears rolling down like they'll never stop.

This is pure sadness, raw and unfiltered. It's not performative, not calculating—just the simple, visceral reaction to losing something wonderful they were certain was theirs.

If you've witnessed this—or been the parent in this situation—you know what usually happens next. There's the rush to console, to fix, to make the sadness go away. *It's okay, sweetheart,* comes the soothing voice. *We'll get you another ice cream.* And sure enough, the tears subside, the promise is fulfilled, a new cone is in hand, and the sadness is forgotten.

Surely, this must be love at its best. Sadness arises, so we rush in with a solution. Sadness out, joy in. It's a perfect exchange.

Or is it?

It's true that offering something a child wants can quickly distract from their sadness. But is distraction the same as joy? Does rushing to replace what's lost truly bring healing, or does it simply postpone the sadness for another day?

INTENTIONS AND MOTIVES

Let's talk about motives. If a parent swiftly replaces a dropped ice cream with the primary intention of bringing their child joy, we might agree this is an act of love. But is it a strategy that works every time a child feels sad, disappointed, or upset? While occasionally stepping in to replace a lost treasure won't harm a child, it's worth examining other possible motives behind this action—motives that might make this approach less effective over time.

For instance, a parent might replace the ice cream simply to stop the tears, not genuinely to bring joy. Many adults, consciously or not, are uncomfortable with children's crying. When they encounter tears, they focus on stopping the crying rather than addressing the sadness behind it. Their actions aim to remove the outward signs of distress rather than truly bring comfort and joy to the situation.

Why does this happen? I'd wager it stems from how those adults' own tears were met in childhood. Perhaps their crying was hushed or dismissed. Maybe they were told to stop crying, reassured it wasn't a big deal, or even threatened with something to *really cry about*. Or perhaps they, too, were distracted by a replacement ice cream.

INTERROGATE THE MOTIVES BEHIND YOUR ACTIONS

We've all known parents who wonder why their best efforts with their children don't seem to bear good fruit. Perhaps we've been one of those parents. In these moments, it can be powerful to examine motives, not just the surface reasons for our actions, but the deeper intentions that drive our behaviour towards our children. Taking this uncomfortable journey can reveal truths that are as sobering as they are transformative. Sometimes, these hidden motives hold the key to understanding why our children seem to be moving in directions we'd rather they didn't.

Parenting expert Dr Becky Kennedy puts it this way: *Your children will remember your intention, not your intervention.* This insight highlights why our unexamined motives matter so much. Even when we believe we are acting out of love, our children can sense when we are motivated by frustration, control, or even a desire to manage our own discomfort rather than truly connecting with them. When our subconscious motives are misaligned with the values we want to instil, the impact on our children can be very different from what we intended.

Dr Kennedy has popularised the idea that all children (and adults) are *good inside*—that even when behaviour is messy or maddening, it's driven by an unmet need or emotional overload, not malice. While I might word that differently as a Christian—I believe we're good *and* flawed, made in God's image, but also capable of missing the mark—I still find her insights into connection and emotional safety enormously helpful.*

I recall the time in my life when God was helping me confront my reactions and motives, particularly when my children were crying. It was a deeply revealing process, a mirror held up to my limits—limits to my compassion, to my patience, and to my ability to bring joy where there was sadness. These truths were discomfiting but necessary, helping me to grow as a parent and as a person.

* For more from Dr Becky Kennedy, see her book *Good Inside: A Guide to Becoming the Parent You Want to Be* (2022), or her TED Talk, *The Most Powerful Parenting Strategy You're Not Using*. Both are accessible and practical resources for parenting through big feelings while maintaining connection.

Consider all the tears that come with childhood's endless stream of little accidents: a spilt drink, a scraped knee, or the inevitable tumble from a bike. It's all part of growing up. Often, these moments of distress could have been avoided. Sometimes, the child has been warned:

Don't climb that tree.

Be careful on the trampoline.

You're going to hurt yourself if you keep horsing around like that.

But the warnings go unheeded, and the tears inevitably arrive. As parents, we're often torn between frustration and sympathy. The instinct might be to scold:

I told you this would happen.

Or to soothe quickly:

You're fine. Come on, let's get you cleaned up.

Here, have a biscuit.

Don't cry—it's not that bad.

But when we take a closer look at our reactions, we might find something deeper driving them: our discomfort with the messiness of sadness, pain, or failure.

Even the most mundane childhood mishaps—cutlery slipped from little hands, a too-exuberant bounce on a trampoline, or a wobble on an uneven surface—can trigger something in us. Why? It could be because they remind us of how fragile life is and how unpredictable it is. And this can frighten us. Then, instead of sitting with the sadness or acknowledging our fear, we might rush to soothe or distract, not out of love, but out of our own unease.

FINDING AN INNER CHILD

Often, the roots of this unease lie in our own childhoods, shaped by how our parents responded to us. In my case, there was little space for sadness or pain when I was growing up. Tears or mistakes often led to a telling-off or a harsh word. So, when my children cried, it activated something in me that felt strangely familiar—a part of me that seemed stuck in childhood, bracing for the kind of reaction I'd once expected from my mother or father.

As I began to explore this, I identified a part of myself that felt an almost desperate need to *warn* me of potential criticism. When I sat with this part of me, it became clear that it was as though an inner child was running up and down inside me, shrieking in fear and waving her hands in warning. I came to call her *Alarm Child.*

Alarm Child was trying to protect me, to shield me from the pain of disapproval I had learned to expect. But the fear she generated wasn't helpful anymore—it only added to the tension I felt in those moments with my children. So, I set about befriending her. I thanked her for her warnings, for her vigilance, and reassured her that things were different now. She didn't need to sound the alarm anymore. Over time, I began to understand that the language of *defects of character* and the language of *parts that don't serve us anymore* are really one and the same. I am comfortable with both. Today, Alarm Child and I are friends, and most of the time, she is quiet.

This is all consistent with Internal Family Systems (IFS) theory, which suggests that these parts of us can still carry the emotional weight of our past. In certain moments, it wasn't just my children's sadness I was reacting to—it was my own buried emotions.

Without realising it, I was parenting not only my child but also the younger version of myself—one who had never been given space for her sadness or mistakes. This is why children remember not just what we do but the deeper intention behind it.

When I looked honestly at my own parenting, I saw how much my fears—of disapproval, of messiness, of lack of control—were shaping my interactions with my children. The more I became aware of this, the more I could shift from controlling or correcting their emotions towards truly holding space for them. Recognising this dynamic was a painful but liberating step towards breaking the cycle and learning to respond to my children with greater compassion and presence.

DISCOVERING HEALING IN SELF-HONESTY

Recognising how my children's tears activated these unresolved parts of myself was a powerful revelation. I vividly recall a moment during a healing workshop when the facilitator said, "The minute I hold *you* responsible for the wound in *my* memory, I'm in trouble." Something inside me clicked. I began to understand that many of my uncomfortable feelings in the present weren't solely about the moment at hand—they were also about the past. This realisation allowed me to detach more from the immediate emotional storm. I could stop blaming the present moment or my loved ones for what I now understood as echoes of old wounds. It was incredibly freeing.

Through the lens of IFS, I began to understand that the feelings I felt today weren't just about the present moment—they were reverberations of my own childhood experiences. Understanding this dynamic was only the first step. What came next was much harder: confronting the ways these unresolved feelings shaped my reactions to my children and then walking in the practice of integrating this awareness and changing my behaviour.

These complex and deeply personal dynamics weren't something I understood all at once. At first, I just couldn't see the patterns or connect my reactions to their deeper roots. It was only through personal reflection, moments of prayer, some moments of sudden grace, and uncomfortable self-examination that the pieces began to fall into place. Gradually, I saw ever more deeply how my childhood experiences had shaped my instinctive responses to my children, often in ways I hadn't realised. Then, I became able to let those responses go.

It is still a little sad for me to admit that in my earliest years as a mother, my immediate response to my children's tears, especially when I had already warned them or asked them to stop, was often anger. Instead of offering comfort, I wanted to tell them off or reprimand them. Impatience drove me to point out their mistakes as if that would somehow make the situation better. Beneath the anger was a mix of emotions: fear for their injuries and irritation that they hadn't listened to me.

When I began to drill down into my motives, what I uncovered wasn't pretty. My reactions weren't about helping my children—they were entirely self-seeking. I was consumed by thoughts like *Why don't they listen to me? Why do they always do what they want? Why won't they let me help them?* Even worse, there was a layer of self-pity: *Now look what I have to deal with. Now look what's happened.*

In those moments, I realised I had little instinct to bring joy to sadness or comfort to pain. My primary goal wasn't to help my children heal—it was simply to make a difficult situation disappear. And my strategies for doing so were, at best, unhelpful: "I told you so!" "Don't do it again!" "Maybe next time you'll listen to me!" These words, though cathartic at the moment, only deepened the disconnection between us.

Even though I could see how damaging my behaviour was (and this is an understatement), I often felt powerless against the tidal wave of emotions—fear, anger, and even rage—that swept through me when my children had an accident.

SITTING WITH UNCOMFORTABLE REALITIES

It was painstaking to uncover how encountering joy was so uncomfortable for me that I could be a killjoy. Just as my parents had with me, I used to point out to my own children how tears and sadness would surely follow if this delight continued unchecked. American academic Brené Brown has documented a widespread tendency among women in the U.S. to live with a pervasive sense of fear—an ever-present feeling of impending doom—that, although life is good right now, it could all disappear in an instant. Something terrible might happen at any moment.*

In my childhood, this same idea was captured in the refrain: Too much laughing ends up crying. I must have heard this expression hundreds of times in my first decade. I had no idea then that this repetition was creating a neural superhighway in my brain—a reflexive fear of joy and an instinctive disconnection from the emotional reality of others. It made it almost impossible for me to comfort my children when they were hurting, especially if I deemed their hurt to have been avoidable.

I vividly recall sitting on my hands in my bedroom, biting my tongue, as I watched my two children jump onto the bed from a chair, wrestle, and squeal with delight. I desperately wanted to stop them. In my mind, I was already imagining the bumps and bruises, the tears, and—more daunting—the fear of how I would manage to comfort them.

But little by little, God worked in me, softening my heart, and helping me face the uncomfortable truth: I had been killing joy because I didn't know how to risk the vulnerability of connection. I wanted to avoid the messiness of my children's pain and my own

---

* In *Daring Greatly* (2012), Brené Brown explores the idea that when things are going well, many people—especially women—struggle to fully experience joy because they're bracing themselves for disaster. She calls this phenomenon "foreboding joy", a form of vulnerability we often resist by rehearsing tragedy.

discomfort in trying to console them. Over time, I learned to stop controlling joy out of fear and instead began to engage with my children, even when the inevitable bumps and bangs happened.

With practice, I discovered what true connection in these moments required: pulling them close, hugging and kissing them, rubbing the sore spot, and acknowledging their pain. I would say things like, "There, there, it's going to be all right." And that future tense, by the way, is important. Don't say *You're all right* when your child quite clearly isn't! It wasn't rocket science, but it may as well have been, given how difficult I found it at first.

It's a delicate thing, bringing joy where there is sadness. Do it too soon, and it can backfire. Is there any more cringeworthy example of this than the well-meaning but poorly timed *They've gone to a better place,* or *It was God's will* said to someone who has just lost a loved one?

The Sadness of Grief

Grief is an intense sadness, and there are no rules on how to handle it perfectly. I learned that genuine comfort requires connection—truly seeing the person in their pain, sitting with them in it, and offering words or gestures that honour their grief. Often, what appears to be well-meaning isn't. Tired clichés like *It's for the best* tend to fall flat because they are disconnected from the grieving person's emotional reality.

Why do we rely on these expressions? Because they make *us* feel better. Say, *It was God's will*, and you might feel you've offered something meaningful. You can tell yourself you're a good person, that you've done your part to console someone. You might even feel pride, believing you've navigated an awkward moment skilfully.

But what's often missed is that these platitudes can deepen disconnection. The grieving person may smile politely, sparing your feelings, but inside, they're brimming with frustration or hurt. Instead of feeling seen or understood, they feel dismissed. And if we've all been in their shoes—hiding our upset to protect someone else's feelings—then how often have we been the ones opening our mouths and inserting our feet?

Grief isn't always about death. Any loss can bring with it a profound sense of sadness. I learned this acutely when my daughter applied to the University of Cambridge. She made it as far as an interview, but then the offer from Trinity College, which she so desperately wanted, didn't come. Everyone—friends, teachers, family, even her frenemies—had been (secretly) expecting her success. This turned out to make the disappointment all the harder to bear.

Facing the well-intentioned but overused expressions of comfort that followed was one of the hardest things she's ever done. Too few people were able to simply say, *I'm sorry*, or acknowledge how deeply disappointed she must have been. Almost without exception, they wanted to offer her comfort without acknowledging her grief. Accompanying her through that loss, I saw how important it was to leave space for her grief, to sit with her pain for as long as she needed, and to wait patiently for the moment when she was ready to see the light at the end of the tunnel.

What was impressive was how quickly she began to make space for tentative positivity. Even on the first day of the bad news, there were glimmers of hope as she spoke about new possibilities. Over the days and weeks that followed, she gradually processed the experience, returning now and then to moments of sorrow but also finding silver linings. This back-and-forth is natural, though parents sometimes mistakenly believe that a loss or sadness can be handled in a *one-and-done* sort of way. The truth is, big disappointments take time to fully integrate. Children may revisit their grief multiple times, alternating between sadness and optimism, as they work towards resolution.

Encouraging her to be compassionate towards those who tried to comfort her too soon and to graciously accept their efforts was no small feat. But we did it together. And in doing so, we drew on all the times we'd practised leaning into sadness before.

THE OTHER END OF THE SPECTRUM

So far, we have been considering the person who rushes to bring optimism and positivity to a sad situation too soon. But at the other end of the spectrum is the person who lingers in sadness, sometimes for far too long. This person seems to lose sight of the many reasons there are to be joyful, even in the midst of pain.

With young children, this tendency often manifests as tantrums and tears that go on and on and on. Or perhaps you've encountered an older child who takes ages to move past the small disappointments and sadness that are commonplace in life. These children may have been blessed with parents who avoid rushing them out of their feelings. However, in their well-meaning desire to validate their child's emotions, these parents may have fallen into a different trap: watering their child's sadness with so much attention that it grows unchecked.

This imbalance creates a different form of disconnection, though it's harder to recognise at first. The parent may feel deeply connected to their child in the moment, but by failing to guide them out of their misery, they are unintentionally fostering an unhelpful emotional dependency. The child becomes stuck in their sadness, unable to move on or recognise the light at the end of the tunnel.

In *The Boy Crisis*, author and psychologist Warren Farrell describes how the virtue of empathy can be taken to such an extreme that it becomes a vice. This resonated deeply with me as I reflected on my daughter's early years. I eventually realised that my empathy for her sadness, while well-intentioned, was doing her no favours.

Once again, God worked in me, showing me the importance of balance. Comforting her was crucial, but so was helping her move on. If I only comforted her without guiding her forward, I was failing her. True connection required both: acknowledging her sadness and pointing her towards the joy and resilience that could follow.

EMPLOYING EMPATHY, NOT FEAR

How do you discover if you are overusing empathy? Examine your motives. Does there come a point when you think your child should be over this by now, but you keep it to yourself? Are you holding back from saying something upbeat and positive? Are you failing to point out reasons why your child could move beyond their sadness or things they could be grateful for? Are you afraid of your child's reaction if you speak up?

If this is the case, you've shifted from a motive of love, where empathy begins, to a motive of fear. Now, you're being nice, not kind. This is where disconnection can creep in. By prioritising your comfort or fear over authentic guidance, you may inadvertently foster emotional dependency instead of growth.

This scenario also reflects a misunderstanding of the biblical warning, *Spare the rod and spoil the child.* One oversimplified—and now largely rejected—interpretation is that parents must physically discipline their children to raise them properly. In reaction, many modern parents have gone to the opposite extreme, attempting to raise children without any form of discipline at all. This is understandable, given how poorly discipline is often practised.

But discipline doesn't mean punishment. To discipline a child means to guide them in the right direction, and the *rod* symbolises this guidance. Just as a shepherd uses a crook to lead sheep rather than beat them, parents can use a metaphorical rod to gently point their children towards peace and joy or block paths that lead to harm.

Our words can serve as this rod, leading a child out of sadness and back to joy. I'm not saying a child who has been crying a moment before must be brimming with happiness the next. I'm saying that after bringing comfort for an appropriate time, parents can nudge their child towards joy. This is not about forcing happiness. God doesn't force us in any direction; he merely guides us.

Occasionally, it feels as though God is blocking us. Nothing works out, and every path seems closed. In those moments, I understand God to be protecting me from choices that would lead to harm. Sometimes, it feels like he's yanking me back from a precipice. More often, he leaves a subtle warning: *Caution.* Sometimes, he doesn't warn at all because the wisdom of the Ten Commandments is already written in our hearts.

We can take our lead from God when guiding our children. What is most appropriate for the situation? Consider the age and temperament of your child. How often have you taught this lesson before? Does your child need a gentle reminder or a deeper explanation about not staying in sadness too long?

For example, giving yet another lecture on gratitude after a teenager misses out on a coveted role in a school play will likely provoke eye-rolling, whether visible or invisible. Instead, listening patiently and then offering a quiet word of encouragement may be far more effective. Or perhaps no word at all.

Many parents struggle with this balance. If we fail to approach sadness thoughtfully, we risk pushing our children away. When children feel dismissed or lectured every time they share their feelings, they stop sharing. For sensitive children, it might take only a few poorly timed lectures before they clam up entirely.

This creates a heartbreaking disconnection. If you believe your child is never sad and that they simply don't experience the struggles other kids do, this could be a sign that they've stopped sharing their inner world with you. No one is immune to sadness—not in the history of humanity. If you don't know what has upset your child this week, you're not off the hook—you've just been left out of the loop.

THE EMPATHY GAP AND ITS CONSEQUENCES

In recent years, we've begun to hear more about the empathy gap—a phenomenon where women find it hard to accept that men experience emotional hurt. It has become commonplace to hear some version of the claim that men are emotionally shut down, stunted, or even that they do not experience emotions at all.

Rather than eliciting compassion, this perception often sparks anger, contempt, or frustration in the person making it, who, more often than not, is a woman. Beneath this anger often lies a self-centred motive: *Because he is emotionally stunted, he cannot love me the way I want to be loved.* Sometimes, it's an even more self-serving belief: *he cannot love me the way I deserve to be loved.*

Another idea I hear frequently is that *He is completely non-empathic.* Yet, ironically, these declarations often come from women who seem to have no compassion for their partner's struggle with empathy. It's a glaring case of the pot calling the kettle black, but it can be difficult to help women see this.

Why? For decades, women have been steeped in the narrative that they are innately superior to men, particularly in the emotional realm. Personally, I don't buy it. I know scores of men who feel deeply misunderstood by their partners. How could that be if women are so wise and emotionally adept?

Interestingly, many men seem to accept or even reinforce this narrative, perhaps for cultural reasons. How often do we hear men, jokingly or otherwise, say things like, *She's the boss*, *I just do what I'm told*, or *I'd be lost without her—she does everything for the kids?* While such statements may seem light-hearted, they subtly affirm the destructive illusion that women are the natural leaders of the family while men are merely supporting players.

This dynamic is reinforced by the ever-present *clueless Dad* trope—the idea that fathers are well-meaning but ultimately incompetent parents. We see it in sitcoms, adverts, and casual conversation: the bumbling dad who can't pack a lunchbox properly or the hapless father who *babysits* his own children, as if this were a favour, not a responsibility.

Men may believe they are being humorous or gracious when they lean into these ideas, but in doing so, they fail to challenge a narrative that ultimately harms both partners and their children. It weakens fathers' roles in the home, overburdens mothers, and models an unbalanced family dynamic for the next generation.

Brené Brown has done us a great service in uncovering an unspoken paradox here. She describes how women often claim to want their partners to be more in touch with their emotions.

Yet when their partners make even tentative attempts to step off the metaphorical white horse or remove their protective armour, it's the women who demand they put it back on.[8]

Men's feelings—especially vulnerability, fear, or weakness—seem intolerable to many women. When a man expresses fear, the woman may feel terrified herself, and her reaction pushes him back into his emotional prison. Women deny this dynamic, but men know it to be true.

Where does this leave us? It points to a fundamental disconnection, where each partner struggles to meet the other's emotional needs. While this section focuses on a dynamic I have observed primarily among women, it's important to recognise that empathy gaps can go both ways. Men, too, play a role in perpetuating these dynamics when they humour or accept narratives that reinforce emotional hierarchies.

This reflection is especially important for those of us raising children because how we speak about our partners, whether mothers or fathers, shapes how our children view the opposite sex. If we model anger, contempt, or dismissal towards a partner or our partner's entire sex, our children will carry those perceptions into their own relationships. Just as a partner may feel misunderstood, a child may one day feel disconnected from a parent who harboured such negativity.

What kind of emotional legacy are we leaving for the next generation?

JUST LISTEN

A friend of mine volunteers in the Chaplaincy of a women's prison. One day, a prisoner who was known to be difficult, violent, and vulnerable came to the Chaplaincy in a state of distress. No one was available to talk to her except my friend, who felt completely inadequate—and more than a little afraid—to step in.

She thought: *I'm not qualified for this.* She wasn't a vicar, priest, chaplain, therapist, doctor, or psychiatrist. She told the woman something like, "I'm not sure I'll be able to help you." But since she was the only one around, she sent up a quick prayer for help, went quiet, and started to listen.

Not knowing what to say, she said nothing. The lady, still agitated, talked for about 30 minutes, pouring out her thoughts and feelings. When she was finished, she thanked my friend and left.

The next day, this same prisoner arrived at the Chaplaincy for a group session in a completely different frame of mind. Her dark, dangerous mood had lifted, replaced by an upbeat and positive energy. She told anyone who would listen how much my friend had helped her the day before.

My friend was stunned and humbled. "I did nothing and said nothing," she told me. "How could it have been me who helped her?"

As she shared this story with me and another friend who works in the therapeutic field, he gave me a knowing glance. We both recognised the power of empathy in action. By sending up that quick prayer and being willing to simply listen, my friend had given the lady exactly what she needed: to be heard.

This act of humility—responding to God's grace and having the courage to say nothing—revealed a profound truth. Sometimes, a person in pain doesn't need advice, solutions, or words. They just need to be heard. And in that space of being truly listened to, their sadness can begin to shift, making way for joy once again.

My friend didn't know she was being empathetic that afternoon in prison. She thought she was doing nothing. But as this story shows, listening without judgement or interruption is often one of the greatest gifts we can offer.

SADNESS, SILENCE AND JOY

In my work with parents, I've noticed something striking: most parents today know they are meant to be empathic. But when I ask them to describe what they say and do in difficult moments with their children, they rarely talk about empathy. Instead, they describe themselves as giving lots of direction, explanation, education, and advice.

So, I offer them a different perspective: empathy is often silent—or, at most, monosyllabic. I point them to the movie *Little Miss Sunshine* and the scene where the little sister sits beside her brother after he receives devastating news. His dream of becoming a pilot is shattered because he's colourblind. She doesn't lecture him, offer solutions, or even speak. Instead, she wordlessly places her head on his shoulder, sharing in his grief.

This simple act of silent presence is profoundly empathic. She brings comfort just by being there with him.

It is said that we have two ears and one mouth for a reason—to remind us to listen twice as much as we speak. This is wise advice indeed. Personally, I know how hard it is to follow. I often finish an interaction with one of my children, wishing I had spoken less and listened more. Practising being quiet is an ongoing effort for me, and it's a challenge I offer to all parents: speak less, listen more, especially when your child is sad.

When we choose silence, we offer connection. We allow space for sadness to be felt, and in doing so, we pave the way for healing. In a mysterious way, sadness will often give way to joy when it is left alone. This isn't something we can force or explain; it is simply how God made us.

When we resist the urge to fix, explain, or rush sadness away, we show our children that their emotions are valid and that they are not alone. This is empathy at its best—an act of quiet, loving connection.

So, in those moments when words feel inadequate, consider saying nothing at all. Instead, be present. Let the silence do its work, and trust that sadness, when acknowledged, can transform into joy.

10

Seek to Console Rather Than Be Consoled

Feelings are contagious. If you're around someone enough, you might catch whatever feeling they're experiencing. If you feel happy and upbeat, that will have a knock-on positive effect on the people around you.

At the same time, of course, the reverse is also true. If someone is feeling down, then that will ultimately have a dispiriting effect on the folks around them. And we have known this instinctively long before today's neuroscience proved it with brain scans.[9]

Interestingly, our language reflects this phenomenon—we talk about certain people being *downers*, and entire books have been written about those who seem to drain others of energy. We intuitively understand this dynamic, which leads to an uncomfortable truth: many of us struggle to console others because we absorb their emotions too easily. If they feel bad, we start to feel bad, and before long, we're the ones in need of comfort.

In response, we often resort to ineffective strategies. One common approach is to soothe *ourselves* rather than the person in distress, offering sympathy that swiftly brushes their sadness aside. Another is simply to listen while they go on (and on…) about their woes—this can be helpful if the listener has strong internal and external boundaries. But if they are too porous, emotional contagion takes hold, and instead of offering solace, the listener ends up feeling just as miserable or resentful as the person they were trying to help.

THE DRAIN OF DUMPING

One psychological term for this type of interaction is *dumping*: the speaker offloads their uncomfortable feelings onto someone else. In other words, a transfer of energy takes place. As a result, the speaker may feel better after the conversation, but the listener doesn't. Or worse, both can end up feeling terrible because the conversation doesn't actually discharge the speaker's negative emotions, and the listener picks up their mood anyway.

This brings to mind the days when I used to collect my daughter after school in her early years. Nia was almost always in a bad mood when I picked her up; she would immediately launch into the woes of her day, and, given her temperament, she tended to mask sadness and upset with anger and irritation. She also has very *big* feelings and *a lot* of persistent energy—a potent combination at the best of times, but particularly when crammed into the confined space of a not-very-big car.

Even though I always started with the best of intentions—excited to see her after the enforced separation of the school day—by the time we got home, I'd be utterly drained.

As I also had a tendency to cover sadness and upset with the more powerful—and therefore, for me, more comfortable—feelings of irritation and anger, it, unfortunately, didn't take long before I was feeling exactly as Nia was feeling: sad, upset, irritated, and angry.

It was not a good situation, and it happened five times a week during term time.

It really didn't help that I had no effective template for consolation from my own childhood. While I tried my best to comfort both Nia and myself, I had little from my own experience to draw on, which left me at a disadvantage. However, theoretically, I knew what I ought to do—sort of.

I knew I ought to listen and allow her to have her feelings. I had worked hard to develop some internal and external boundaries, so I didn't *immediately* catch whatever feelings she brought to the car. I knew about making empathic noises like *oh, uh-huh, oh dear,* and *sounds hard*. But it was still tricky because, unlike in the parenting books I read—or in the case of plenty of my clients' children—my own daughter didn't seem to discharge her emotions after five, ten, or even twenty minutes or more of empathic listening.

In the end, I wasn't a big enough container for her feelings. Sometimes, I blew it by snapping at her when my patience ran out. Other times, my worry rather than my anger got the upper hand, and I *parent-whined* back at her. My worry was, I think, fairly realistic because I couldn't shake the concern that all this lovely positive parental attention for her bad mood might actually be reinforcing the very behaviour I was trying to soothe.

WHEN EMPATHY BACKFIRES

In other words, by listening so long and so well, I was inadvertently turning my daughter into a whiner. Because of the rules of reinforcement: *what you pay attention to, you get more of.* From a child's point of view, of course, it makes perfect sense to do more of what attracts such high-value attention. I started to think of empathy as a riskier strategy than I had before, recognising that it cannot be used indiscriminately.

It is possible for this virtue to become a vice, so there needs to be a limit to what we listen to. And why? Because all human beings actually have limits! Shall I say that again? *It is necessary to limit what you will listen to because all human beings have limits.*

I am now convinced that the widespread advice to *listen to our children and let them have their feelings* has been disastrous for a significant minority, particularly for children like my daughter, who have such big feelings that they cannot be contained by a mere human parent. It hasn't been great advice for less-spirited children either; many have simply become whiny and negative because they have not been well-counselled in difficult situations.

At some point, I realised that listening is only part of consoling. My faith in gentle attachment parenting had begun to waver. I could see that, while my intentions were loving, they were not effective. The moment I reclaimed some of the behaviourist principles I had abandoned, I became a more honest, loving, and effective parent, and Nia became a noticeably happier child.

As I struggled to find a balance at home, therapists working with traumatised clients were making similar discoveries. In the relatively early days of treating PTSD, counsellors were sent to disaster zones to encourage survivors to talk about their experiences, based on the belief that talking about the event would prevent long-term trauma. Unfortunately, this practice sometimes had an unintended effect. Talking without the right context or support ran the risk of leaving people more traumatised, not less.

Eventually, the professional therapeutic world learned that effective consultation requires more than just allowing people to talk. While it is crucial to let people express their feelings, it is equally important to gently guide them towards recognising that the danger has passed and that they are safe now.* This delicate process—acknowledging pain while fostering a sense of closure—is far easier said than done.

Though my experiences with Nia were not on the scale of trauma, they taught me this same lesson in a thousand smaller ways. Consolation, whether in the face of everyday challenges or devastating loss, requires more than empathy. It demands boundaries, perspective, and the ability to create a space where feelings can be held without overwhelming either person.

A LESSON IN DIVINE COMFORT

Learning once again from God, I am reminded of something that happened while I was on a skiing holiday with my family one spring. I was a novice skier at the time—only in my second year

* EMDR (Eye Movement Desensitisation and Reprocessing) and Somatic Experiencing are trauma therapies that support individuals in processing overwhelming experiences. Both approaches aim to reduce the emotional intensity of traumatic memories and restore a felt sense of safety in the body.

of learning. Day one was going well, but by lunchtime, one of my feet had started to hurt in the ski boot. Still, I pressed on.

By the end of the day, I was in terrible pain, and every turn was mildly agonising. When I finally got off the mountain and eased my feet into slippers, the relief was immense. I was pleased to see that the big toe on my left foot was clearly bruised—proof that I wasn't just being dramatic.

By the next morning, the bruise was even more spectacular, and I couldn't fit my foot into most of the shoes I had with me. I spent the day mooching around the very pretty Italian town at the foot of the mountain, drinking terrible tea and wishing, for the umpteenth time, that I drank coffee.

The following day, my toe still wouldn't go into a shoe, never mind a ski boot, and I began to realise I might not be able to ski again on this trip. The reactions from our large group were interesting—plenty of pitiful looks, lots of awkward silences. People didn't seem to know what to say. I took myself into town again, exploring the churches and cafés, keeping my chin up. I certainly wasn't as upset as people expected me to be, but I was slightly mystified by how important it seemed to everyone to get me back on the slopes.

On day four, I decided to go up the mountain anyway, book in hand, to find a café on the ski hill. Between the pain in my foot and missing out on the glorious spring skiing, I was feeling a little despondent. I was also getting thoroughly fed up with all the well-meaning attempts to console me—reassurances (against all the evidence) that I'd surely be skiing again that afternoon, endless suggestions for reducing the pain, adjusting ski boots, bandaging toes, and so on.

And as I smiled and nodded through yet another well-intentioned attempt to fix things, I realised why all this supposed consolation was leaving me feeling worse. As we explored in the previous chapter on sadness and joy, we don't just react to what is said—we react to the intention behind it. Too many of my consolers weren't truly trying to comfort me; I could sense their real goal was to ease their own awkwardness or make my inconvenient injury go away.

So, I made my way up the mountain, determined to enjoy my book in the sunshine on a café veranda. I arrived at a pretty little chalet housing a café-restaurant and stepped inside. As I walked through the front door, feeling a bit sorry for myself as the reality of a ski-less week fully dawned on me, I caught the strains of a beloved piece of music playing from the speakers.

I almost wanted to cry. In that moment, I knew this was something special, something arranged just for me by the God of the universe. I was Hagar, and he was *the God who sees me*

(Genesis 16:13). He knew my disappointment, my sadness, and my efforts to stay cheerful, to not let this setback spoil my holiday.

He knew I wasn't complaining or whining. But he also knew I was feeling low, that I'd rather not have a throbbing toe, that I would much prefer to be out on the slopes, still trying to learn to ski. And that, more than anything, I would rather be spending the day with my family and friends instead of wandering around alone with my books.

Then, after that, the first song ended (I think it was something by Louis Armstrong or maybe Ella Fitzgerald), and another favourite was played. And then another. My heart surged with joy. Once again, I experienced so tangibly that I am beloved by the God of the whole universe. He who threw stars into space cared enough about *me* and my mood to remind me that he loved me, that he saw me, and that, yes, he knew I was hurting—but really, it was all okay.

He did it with music, sunshine, and impeccable timing. I'll never forget the moment, even if I've forgotten the exact songs.

This is how one should console. Like God, who makes it clear that *yes, you are hurting, but I am near you. I will not leave you. And it will be okay.*

You'll notice that, in this case, my suffering began with a physical injury and extended into emotional pain. Physical pain almost always brings a psychological reaction that also needs attention. But things get trickier when the hurt in need of consolation is purely psychological. And these are the hurts that large numbers of parents seem to miss.

THE COMPLEX ROLE OF PARENTS IN DEPRESSION AND SUICIDE

Time and again, we hear of parents who are utterly blindsided when their beloved teen or young adult child takes their own life. It is a heartbreaking reality—one that no parent ever wants to imagine. And yet, as painful as it is to acknowledge, suicide does not come out of nowhere. A young person who reaches this point has been suffering deeply, perhaps for a long time, and feels hopeless enough to see no better way forward.

This is *not* to say that parents could have prevented every tragedy, nor to suggest that love alone can ward off the complex and sometimes invisible struggles that lead to suicide. But I do believe we need to have a harder conversation about how deeply a child's sense of belonging and emotional well-being is shaped within the home. Some parents may be emotionally absent or unaware due to neglect or self-absorption, whether because of unresolved trauma, emotional overwhelm, or simply lacking good models, but many others, perhaps the majority, are well-meaning, loving people who have been misled by cultural messages about parenting.

One of the most pervasive of these messages has been the misapplication of gentle parenting. In recent decades, a well-intentioned shift towards emotional attunement and connection has, in many cases, thrown the baby out with the bathwater, prioritising empathy while neglecting the essential role of boundaries, structure, and parental authority.

A lack of loving but firm limits can leave children feeling more anxious, not less, adrift in a world where they sense they have too much power and not enough containment. And yet, paradoxically, the opposite problem can also arise out of the same parenting philosophy: children who grow up feeling overly controlled, not through traditional harsh discipline, but through covert control disguised as connection.

I have seen this time and again in my private practice—children who are deeply loved, whose parents work incredibly hard to *do everything right*, but whose children still feel unheard, unseen, and emotionally burdened. Why? I have a hunch that despite all the attunement and apparently open conversations, there can remain an unspoken expectation: that they become the *perfect child* their parents have painstakingly nurtured them to be.

Some children can be exquisitely sensitive to the subtext of our interactions. A parent may offer long, compassionate lectures about kindness, fairness, and emotional intelligence, *believing this is what they are teaching,* but the child may experience it very differently. Instead of feeling guided, they could feel condescended to, subtly controlled, or burdened with an impossible standard. What was meant as a connection starts to feel like an expectation to perform emotional maturity beyond their years.

Often, it's because the parent is carrying too much—too much pressure to raise a child who turns out well, too much fear of getting it wrong, too much self-doubt from their own wounds and histories. These parents are trying so hard to *do everything right* that they sometimes pass along the very pressure they're drowning in.

The result? A child who is externally compliant but internally struggling, who may smile and nod while privately feeling misunderstood, resentful, or even suffocated by their parents' covert expectations. This kind of emotional mismatch doesn't always lead to visible rebellion or defiance, though it might. In some cases, it leads to something far more concerning: a deep sense of isolation within an outwardly *perfect* family.

It would be deeply unfair to claim that a parent who loses a child to suicide has failed them, and that is not what I am saying. Life is more complicated than that. But I think we need to be honest about the protective role of parental presence, not just in physical closeness, but in emotional availability and authenticity. A teenager whose need for belonging is well met within their family and community, who has a strong felt sense of being loved, is far less likely to find themselves in a place of utter despair.

And how does a child attain this deep sense of being beloved and belonging? It is something they discover first and foremost within the family through parents who are not only present and loving but who also offer clear guidance, healthy authority, and the emotional honesty to admit when their own needs and expectations are getting in the way of true connection.

THE HIDDEN COSTS OF EMOTIONAL DISCONNECTION IN FAMILIES

I recently watched *Our Souls At Night*, a film starring Jane Fonda and Robert Redford as an elderly widow and widower, each struggling with their relationships with their grown children while figuring out how to create a more supportive intimacy with each other.

It was heartbreaking to watch Fonda's character, who, despite being charming in her interactions with her neighbour, was utterly at a loss when it came to her adult son. She simply did not know how to support him in the grief he still felt over the loss of his sister many years before.

More than that, she was perplexed by his deep pain. The film captured something painfully true: the suffering that unfolds when parents and children fail to connect in meaningful ways, leaving both parties hurting, often for years.

Yet, as much as I was moved by the film's portrayal of this dynamic, I also found myself frustrated. The film seemed, at times, to excuse or minimise the mother's cluelessness. This may be unfair of me—I am not an unbiased critic. I have been the wounded adult child of imperfect parents, but my children are still relatively young. I have never been the bewildered parent of an estranged adult child. So, when I watched the son lashing out in pain, I understood his side in a way that I couldn't fully access for his mother.

That said, Fonda's fictional son was so unrelentingly cruel to her that I couldn't help but bristle as a mother myself. And yet, I found myself thinking: *Well, no wonder their relationship is a disaster if that's how she handles it.*

As the story unfolds, we come to understand the root of his bitterness: his mother's emotional withdrawal and neglect in the aftermath of his sister's death. It was a tragedy beyond words—a mother is grieving the loss of a child, but it leads her to respond in a way that devastates her relationship with the child who remains.

How often does this happen? More than we might want to admit. Many books have been written by people who lost a sibling in childhood, only to find that, after the funeral, their parents never spoke of them again.

Of course, we must have compassion for parents grieving such an unimaginable loss. And yet, we must also have compassion for the grieving child left behind. If we pretend that a parent's response to tragedy has no lasting impact on their child, we fail those children all over again.

Just as importantly, we fail to honour the parents who *have* navigated such heartbreaking circumstances with grace, awareness, and love. The truth is, not all ways of grieving are equally effective. All may be equally *valid* because grief is profoundly personal. However, not all are equally *effective* when it comes to preserving the emotional well-being of the family.

THE CRUCIAL ROLE OF PARENTS IN EMOTIONAL WELL-BEING

Of course, some parents *do* see that their child is struggling and may spend years fearing the day when their worst nightmare comes true. Families who suffer the tragedy of suicide live with the weight of an incomplete understanding, both in our culture and within the field of mental health, about how to best support those in severe emotional distress.*

We seem to be drawn to the idea that depression is a purely biological illness. I wonder if this is because such an explanation seems to absolve both parents and children of responsibility. And to be clear, I do *not* deny the biological aspect of depression. It is evident that some people have an inborn disposition towards experiencing and staying in depressive states. But it does us all a disservice to downplay the role that parenting and family life play in shaping a child's inner emotional world. If we want to reduce the staggering number of young people dying by suicide, we must acknowledge parents' pivotal role in fostering their child's emotional resilience.

---

* For any parent in this situation, I highly recommend Sophie Scott's book *You Are Not Alone In This: Supporting a Loved One's Mental Health Without Losing Your Own* (2025)

Dr Gabor Maté and Dr Gordon Neufeld, in their book *Hold On to Your Kids: Why Parents Need to Matter More Than Peers*, argue that children's sense of security and emotional grounding comes first and foremost from their attachment to their parents. When parents are attuned to their children, providing consistent connection, listening, and understanding, they create a solid foundation for emotional resilience. However, when that attachment is weakened or replaced by reliance on peers for validation and belonging, children are left vulnerable to emotional instability. As Maté and Neufeld emphasise, the primary role of parents is to be a compass and anchor for their children, fostering a secure sense of identity and self-worth. Without this, children may struggle to navigate the complexities of life, increasing their risk of emotional distress.

If parenting shapes a child's inner world, then it stands to reason that patterns of emotional distress, including depression, are not only inherited but also, at times, learned. And what is learned can, with effort and the right support, be unlearned. This is why Cognitive Behavioural Therapy (CBT) can succeed in treating depression: it directly challenges the thought patterns that keep people trapped in despair. However, CBT is not the only path to relearning. Across different traditions, there are communities dedicated to untangling the past—groups where people work to unlearn the patterns of their childhoods and reshape the way they respond to life's challenges.

CBT works by identifying and reshaping harmful thought patterns, while attachment-focused healing addresses the deeper emotional imprints left by early relationships. Faith, too, plays a vital role for many, offering a source of meaning, belonging, and the assurance that suffering is not endured alone. These different approaches are not mutually exclusive but can work together to help individuals break free from cycles of despair.

GRIEF, LOSS AND THE CONSOLATION WE ALL NEED

Beyond the widely accepted understanding of family dynamics within traditional therapies, there exists a deeply engaged therapeutic subculture where the connection between how we were parented and how we turn out is taken with utmost seriousness. In the world of emotional sobriety, for example, individuals confront the wounds and protective patterns shaped by their early family environments—patterns that often manifest as diagnosable mental health issues later in life. Therapeutic communities and multiple fellowships within the 12-step world are dedicated to uncovering and healing these deeply rooted emotional wounds.

For parents, this work is particularly crucial. Unhealed emotional wounds are often unconsciously passed down, shaping the way we respond to our own children's distress. By engaging in a journey towards emotional sobriety ourselves, we not only heal our past but also equip the next generation with healthier patterns of resilience and connection.

These approaches highlight the formative influence of early family environments on mental health and the possibility of transformation. By recognising and addressing these dynamics, individuals and families alike can begin to break cycles of dysfunction for future generations.

Yet, as society grapples with depression, we often turn first to pharmaceutical solutions. While antidepressants have their place and are beneficial for some, a growing body of evidence suggests they are not effective for everyone.[10] For a small minority, especially the under-25s, they may even exacerbate the problem, with reports of increased suicidal ideation as a potential side effect.[11]

This raises important questions about how quickly depression is diagnosed and medicated, particularly in those who are grieving. Grief, after all, is not a disorder but a natural response to profound loss. In many cases, what grieving people need most is not a prescription but genuine consolation—an empathic, human connection that allows them to process their pain and begin to heal.

When we rush to medicalise grief, we risk overlooking its deeper emotional and relational dimensions.

It's not only the grief associated with death that risks being prematurely pathologised. Lesser losses, such as the loneliness that might accompany a job or home relocation, can also lead to feelings of sadness or despair. These are very real emotional responses, but they do not necessarily require a clinical diagnosis or medication.

What such situations often call for is not a prescription but the courage to engage with the underlying issue. Perhaps it's about persevering in the slow and sometimes painful work of integrating into a new community or, conversely, recognising that the move hasn't worked and must be undone. These challenges are best met with relational support, genuine understanding, and a space for honest reflection, not a pill.

By confusing natural emotional responses with pathological conditions, we risk depriving people of the opportunity to address the real sources of their pain. Grief, loneliness, and disappointment are not illnesses to be cured but experiences to be met with consolation and connection.

MASTERING THE GIFT OF CONSOLATION

With all this in mind, it is clear that parents must learn how to console. If we remain the kind of people who primarily seek consolation rather than offer it, if we never develop the ability to provide true solace, we will fail to meet one of our children's deepest needs: connection during sorrow. Learning this skill in adulthood can be slow and painstaking work, but it is essential if we wish to leave behind a legacy that speaks of love and wisdom.

This is not to say we should deny our own need for comfort—far from it. A productive way forward lies in what Jesus taught in the Gospels, what our spiritual forebears, like St. Francis of Assisi, lived out, and what neuroscience confirms about how our brains respond to connection and consolation.

Fortunately, it is truly fulfilling to become the kind of person who can rise above their own discomfort to offer solace to others in need, not by suppressing our own pain or pretending to console when we are, in fact, trying to console ourselves, but by truly being present. The ability to console is the fruit of doing the difficult inner work required to develop the capacity to give, even in the midst of misfortune. If you embrace this challenge, you will become the person everyone turns to at your father's funeral.

Ultimately, true consolation is not about erasing pain but about standing beside those who suffer, bearing witness to their sorrow without flinching. When we offer this kind of love to our children, not rushing to fix or silence their hurt but holding it with them, we give them a gift that will last long beyond childhood. Faith in love itself. A trust that they are never alone. A peace that is not dependent on circumstances but rooted in the unshakable knowledge that they are cherished, no matter what.

11

Seek to Understand Rather Than Be Understood

It is part of the human experience to have a deep-seated need to be understood. This desire is so universal that it seems hardwired into us, written in our hearts, inscribed in our DNA. It's part of how we are made. It shapes how we relate to one another, how we build communities, and even how we seek meaning in faith.

At the heart of understanding lies empathy—a quality that not only meets our need to be understood but also allows us to offer that understanding to others. But empathy is tricky. Despite its prominence in our vocabulary, many people struggle to define it. They might know they should be empathic, but remain unsure how to achieve it. Often, they assume they are empathetic simply because they hope to be compassionate.

Interestingly, while we're often blind to our own lack of empathy, we're keenly aware when others fail to empathise with us. We know we haven't been understood when, instead of feeling better, we feel worse after someone's attempt at empathy. The signs can be subtle: a conversation feels slightly off or falters, the subject abruptly changes, or the other person unwittingly shuts us down. On the surface, all may seem well. But internally, the misunderstood person retreats, creating a barrier between themselves and the one who failed to connect. Such disconnections, though often unnoticed, can carry significant consequences for both individuals and their relationships.

THE CONSEQUENCES OF NON-EMPATHY

Sometimes, the absence of empathy in a conversation is barely perceptible. At other times, a disconnect is undeniable. An exchange spirals into a full-blown argument, marked by raised voices, hurt feelings, and anger on both sides. These moments leave no doubt: the encounter has gone badly. Relationships may suffer lasting damage if misunderstandings are left unresolved.

Psychologists call this rupture and repair—the natural cycle of connection, disconnection, and reconnection that plays out in all relationships. Minor ruptures happen all the time: we snap at someone, misunderstand their intent, and fail to offer the support they need at the moment. But relationships are not broken by rupture alone—they are broken when there is no repair. When misunderstandings are left to fester, when no effort is made to bridge the gap, small disconnects accumulate into resentment and alienation.

This is where many families find themselves stuck—a pattern of misunderstanding, frustration, and conflict. The stereotype of the Christmas family row is all too familiar, reflecting an underlying inability to listen and truly understand each other.

The research on empathy paints a stark picture: our capacity for empathy is rooted in our earliest experiences. As infants and children, we need to feel understood to develop the ability to offer understanding in return. When this fundamental need is unmet, it creates a developmental block. Adults who have not experienced empathy themselves often struggle to offer it to others. Instead, they remain stuck, seeking to be understood rather than learning to understand others.

Studies of neglected children, such as those raised in Romanian orphanages, underscore the devastating consequences of emotional deprivation. These children often suffer severe developmental delays, attachment difficulties, and social withdrawal.[12] By contrast, children who experience empathy and attunement from caregivers are more likely to develop prosocial behaviours, such as kindness and cooperation, as they grow.[13] The seeds of empathy are sown in childhood.

The breakdown of empathy at a personal level—within families and relationships—has wider cultural consequences. When children grow up in environments devoid of empathy and repair, they struggle to navigate conflict in healthy ways. This is not just a private, domestic issue. It has profound implications for how we function as a society. Beneath all our personal and cultural dysfunction lies a longing we all share: the ache to be understood.

THE GIFT OF BEING UNDERSTOOD

I am convinced our need to be understood is one reason why God, as I understand him, came to earth, suffered, and died. How could we come to believe in and draw close to a God who didn't know what it is like to be human? In the person of Jesus, God reveals his intimate knowledge of our deepest struggles: he understands betrayal by a friend, being mocked and bullied. He understands what it is to suffer grave injustice, even to endure physical torture and be put to death.

God the Father knows what it is like to watch a child suffer and die. Part of the beauty of Christianity lies in this truth: we are deeply understood by a God who has suffered and continues to suffer alongside us.

This is one of the most comforting aspects of the Christian faith: it presents a God who truly understands humanity. Far from being distant, he is present—a knowing insider who has walked through the joys and struggles of human life. He had a family, not because *he* needed one to understand *us*—he is God, after all—but because it helps *us* to understand *him*. For Christians, the idea that God became human speaks to the ultimate act of empathy, making his love tangible.

While Christianity offers a meaningful answer to this longing, the comfort of being understood is not limited to faith. There is something truly reassuring about being truly known by someone who has shared similar experiences. Whether in faith, community, or ordinary friendships, this ability to relate brings a strong sense of belonging. This is what makes support groups so powerful—they bring together people with common challenges and create spaces where compassion can flow freely.

Twelve-step groups, in particular, embody this principle. They offer a safe place to speak honestly, be heard without judgment, and receive the gift of understanding from those who've been there, too. Those who share our journey are less likely to dismiss our pain or offer hollow words and much more likely to extend true empathy. In this way, the understanding found in Jesus and the support of the community complement one another, offering a truly holistic sense of belonging and comfort.

For those who have found empathy and deep connection in shared human experiences but have never considered Christianity, the idea of God's empathy may seem unfamiliar or even unnecessary. Yet Christianity presents something unique: the assurance of a divine understanding that is both infinite and personal. The person of Jesus not only walks alongside us in our pain but also offers a source of hope and love that transcends what any human connection alone can provide.

But being understood is only half the story. The real challenge begins when we try to extend that same understanding to others, especially when it's inconvenient, uncomfortable, or undeserved.

THE CHALLENGE OF LIVING EMPATHY

Another overlooked gift of our Judeo-Christian heritage is its role in fostering a deeper understanding of ourselves, of our children, and of our relationships. Christian morality, far from being a rigid set of rules, provides an essential framework for empathy. It teaches us that every person—child or adult—is made in the image of God, worthy of patience, guidance, and love. When we discard this framework, we risk losing not just our moral compass but also our ability to properly understand and nurture one another.

Yet even with this framework, living empathy is hard. Where are the people who truly live out the prayer of St. Francis, seeking to understand rather than be understood? While there are certainly many moments when people show empathy, my impression, as discussed throughout this book, is that many struggle to practice it well, particularly when it's most needed.

And if I'm being honest, I have been one of those people.

I didn't see it at first, but parenting held up a mirror—and what it showed wasn't flattering. I wasn't nearly as empathic as I liked to believe. For years, I had been stuck in a pattern of trying to be understood rather than understanding others. In arguments with my husband or family, I would become like a dog with a bone, unable to let go of my need to be heard. With acquaintances, I would withdraw silently, nursing hurt feelings but never voicing them. My relationships were not in good order, but I couldn't see why—until parenting forced me to truly reflect.

CHANGING SLOWLY

Parenting brought me face-to-face with my empathy deficit. My children needed me to stay in connection with them, permanently. Unlike relationships with adults, where I could retreat or disengage, I couldn't walk away from my children. Even in moments of frustration, I was compelled to reconnect. This desire for ongoing connection was a turning point. I realised that my habitual way of managing relationships—focused on being understood—wouldn't work with my children.

I had always known, at least in theory, that children need empathy for healthy emotional development. I was also painfully aware of the wounds I carried from my own parents' failure to raise me in an empathic way. What I hadn't understood until I became a parent was how deeply ingrained my own empathy deficit was—and how hard it would be to overcome.

At first, I fell into the trap of trying to make my very small children understand me, especially in moments of stress. While I made great efforts to understand them, my capacity to really see their point of view was often overridden by my need to be understood. I thought I understood them, but my reactions, tinged with impatience and even, at times, contempt, betrayed otherwise. I regarded their thinking as wrong and inferior to my own, and I failed to offer them the kind of understanding that *feels like* being understood.

It was only through sheer persistence—and what I believe was God's grace—that I began to change. I recall moments when I felt an almost supernatural patience, a greater ability to see things from my children's perspective, and an uncharacteristic calmness in situations that would have previously overwhelmed me. I believe these periods of grace were God's way of giving me a template for what empathy and patience look like in practice. But this grace was temporary. Sooner or later, I had to learn new habits the normal way—slowly and painfully, through effortful practice.

Bit by bit, I became more understanding of my children. The process was far from easy; it felt like unlearning deeply ingrained patterns while building entirely new ones. Yet even as I began to make progress with my children, making the same changes in my relationship with my husband proved even harder. It took time—much more time—to shift from being consumed with my own perspective to genuinely seeking to understand his. But the struggle was worth it.

Little by little, my relationships healed.

UNDERSTANDING IN RELATIONSHIPS: A VITAL KEY TO HARMONY

It led me to wonder: how many divorces or relationship breakdowns are rooted in the desire to be understood rather than to understand?

In my parenting workshops, when I explain empathy and how it meets our deep need to be seen, heard, and understood, I often use the example of a row with a spouse or partner.

Imagine a heated argument that suddenly resolves—not because your spouse or partner agrees with your perspective, but because they finally understand it. Everyone recognises this moment. The wind goes out of your argumentative sails when you realise you've been understood. With that recognition comes a pause, a space to breathe, and often, a new openness to understanding the other person. Empathy disarms conflict.

This dynamic extends beyond romantic relationships into parenting. Many parents fall into the *if I can only make them understand* trap, spending hours reasoning with children who are simply too young for reason to *work*. This approach rarely succeeds—even with older children—because it assumes that understanding will lead to compliance.

While understanding *can* make a child more inclined to cooperate, it is neither a guarantee nor a requirement for cooperation. If a parent believes otherwise, frustration and resentment are inevitable. Parents who endlessly explain or repeat themselves when faced with non-cooperation often hold unconscious but problematic beliefs: that a child who is asked often enough will eventually comply; that a child who understands the reasoning will do as they ask.

Neither is true.

As a result, parents keep explaining, and children keep resisting. Frustration builds, and even the most patient parent may begin to act in ways that harm the relationship—yelling, withdrawing, or resorting to excessively punitive measures. Over time, this cycle erodes trust and connection, particularly as children grow into teenagers.

Teenagers—both British and American—often say their number one complaint about their parents is that they *just don't understand.*[14] And here's the ironic thing: many parents believe they are deeply understanding because they mistake explaining themselves at length for empathy, but real understanding isn't about making someone see your point of view. It's about seeing theirs.

If you've been accustomed to explaining yourself endlessly, it may feel counterintuitive at first, but I urge you to stop. Instead, focus on understanding your child. This shift will transform your relationship and foster a sense of connection and trust that no amount of reasoning can achieve.

Understanding the Language of Commands and Requests

Here's another subtle but common dynamic I've noticed that often undermines harmony at home. Invariably, parents today begin with requests rather than commands. I understand this tendency—it feels more respectful and more aligned with modern ideals of fairness and partnership. Asking *Will you...?* or *Would you...?* seems kinder than issuing a direct command. So, we say, *Will you set the table, please?* Or *would you like some broccoli?* Instead of *Set the table* or *Eat your broccoli.*

The problem is that when we phrase things as questions, our children hear them as genuine choices. And why wouldn't they? From a child's perspective, it's perfectly reasonable to interpret *Will you set the table?* as a choice between setting the table and not setting the table. Naturally, they often choose not to. After all, whatever they're doing at the moment—whether playing, drawing, or daydreaming—probably seems more fun than setting the table.

Here's where things can go awry. When parents offer what seems like a choice but react with annoyance when their child exercises that choice, children perceive this as unfair. And in this instance, they're right. While many accusations of parental unfairness are unfounded, this one is not.

However, most children won't articulate this feeling. They won't say: *You offered me a choice, so it's unfair that you're upset when I didn't choose what you wanted.* Instead, they'll express their frustration in other ways—often through resistance, defiance, or the dreaded tantrum.

As adults, we can draw on our own experiences of frustration to understand this dynamic. Think of a time when you were upset and couldn't find the right words to express yourself. Perhaps you were trying to explain your perspective to a partner, colleague, or friend, but felt unheard or misunderstood. What did you do? Many of us resort to actions—slamming a door, raising our voice, withdrawing altogether—when words fail us.

Children are no different. Their resistance or defiance often stems from a similar inability to articulate their feelings, leaving their behaviour to speak for them. When we approach a child's misbehaviour with this understanding, we create an opportunity to model the very compassion we want them to develop. Instead of reacting to their resistance with anger or exasperation, we can pause and consider: *What might my child be thinking or feeling that they cannot yet put into words?*

This doesn't excuse the behaviour, but it allows us to address the underlying thoughts and emotions rather than escalate the conflict. It also helps our children feel seen and understood—an experience that builds trust and strengthens the parent-child bond, even as we guide them with firm and clear expectations.

Language matters. If we habitually phrase commands as requests, we create confusion and frustration, and—whether we realise it or not—we weaken our own authority.

PARENTAL AUTHORITY IS REAL

Parenting requires balance. True authority is only effective when it is built on understanding. Parents who genuinely seek to understand their children—their emotions, struggles, and developmental limits—are better equipped to offer guidance that feels both firm and fair. When authority is disconnected from understanding, it becomes harsh; when understanding is disconnected from authority, it becomes weak. The key is integration.

Our parents may not have always got the balance right, but they understood this principle far better than we do now. When we embrace our authority and communicate it clearly, we teach our children valuable lessons about boundaries, respect, and responsibility. This isn't about control or dominance—it's about guidance grounded in love, clarity, and consistency.

I saw this in my own family life. We practised what I call consensus shopping. My daughter and I both had a say in what she wore: she respected that I wouldn't pay for clothes I found inappropriate, and I respected that she wouldn't wear something she disliked. When we reached an impasse, I held my boundary. I explained my reasoning, but ultimately, I decided what got bought.

This balance between authority and respect extends beyond parenting decisions—it shapes how children interact with the world.

Many parents I have worked with struggle when their children insist on wearing sportswear for every occasion, refusing even slightly formal clothing for weddings or family events. It seems trivial, but it's not. Small battles over clothing reflect a much bigger parenting dilemma: whether to choose immediate harmony over teaching long-term lessons in respect and adaptability. Many parents today hesitate to assert authority, fearing they will seem too strict or arbitrary. But in reality, a clear, confident authority is one of the greatest gifts we can give our children.

What Western parents don't tend to realise is that dressing appropriately is not just about pointless rules—it's about respect.

Many non-Western cultures place a strong emphasis on attire as a way to honour traditions, individuals, and occasions. Jeremy Courtney, in *Preemptive Love: Pursuing Peace One Heart at a Time*, describes how living in Iraq deepened his understanding of how small actions, like dressing appropriately, reflect larger values of dignity and community.

This perspective is a valuable reminder: when we insist on appropriate clothing, behaviour, or attitudes, we're not being arbitrary. We're teaching our children how to adapt, how to respect the people and spaces they inhabit, and how to navigate a world where not everything is up for negotiation. And here's where many parents struggle: they don't realise their hesitation to assert authority is actually failing to understand their child's need for it. Without these lessons, we leave children at a disadvantage—not just in the family but in society at large.

It is time to reclaim authority as an essential tool of good parenting, not as a relic of the past, but as a necessary foundation for raising secure, adaptable, respectful, and *happy* human beings.

MORE ABOUT AUTHORITY

Parental authority is widely misunderstood today, particularly in the UK and the US, where it's often dismissed or confused with being authoritarian. Yet it is so essential to the healthy functioning of human society that it is enshrined in the Ten Commandments:

Honour your father and mother, that it may go well with you in this life. (Exodus 20:12)

I wasn't a practising Christian when I first referenced this commandment to my children. But I noticed that invoking it helped them understand why I required certain behaviours. It freed me from the need to justify my authority constantly, allowing me to simply step into my role as their guide.

In my work with parents, I often see how a lack of clarity in authority leads to unnecessary conflict. Parents fear being too strict, but children actually feel safer when they know where they stand. Jordan Peterson, the Canadian psychologist, puts it plainly: *Don't let your children do anything that makes you dislike them.* When parents shy away from authority, it often comes from a misunderstanding of empathy, as if being empathic means never setting boundaries. However, true understanding recognises that children need guidance, not endless negotiation. If parents abdicate their role, children will subconsciously step into it themselves, and this is deeply unsatisfying for them. They may seem victorious at the moment, but their sense of security is compromised.

A home without clear parental authority is not a democratic utopia—it's a source of deep insecurity for a child who needs to know their parent is firmly in charge. Such homes often become deeply fractious and exhausting for parents, too.

I see this constantly in my parenting classes, private practice, and in my own experience as a parent: rather than embracing a true authoritative parenting with a balance of warmth and firm boundaries, many parents today swing wildly between *permissive* and *authoritarian* approaches. These terms come from psychologist Diana Baumrind's influential model of parenting styles, which distinguishes between permissive (all warmth, no limits), authoritarian (all limits, no warmth), and balanced, *authoritative* styles.[15]

This isn't just exhausting—it's ineffective.

Instead of getting the best of both worlds, they get the worst. When they try to be permissive, children feel insecure rather than grateful because they lack guidance. When they suddenly clamp down with harsh discipline, children resent it rather than respect it because it feels arbitrary rather than predictable.

Often, the swing is prompted by burnout: after overusing empathic understanding in an attempt to stay connected, parents find themselves with no fuel left and snap. I know—I've done it myself, mistaking permissiveness for empathy until I hit a wall. But understanding your child doesn't mean indulging every impulse. Sometimes, your role isn't to explain—it's to lead.

While no model captures the full complexity of human behaviour, I've found Baumrind's framework consistently useful. In my experience, authoritative parenting—firm, loving, and consistent—is the best approach.

In the past, parental authority often leaned too far towards control, with responses like *Because I said so* offered as the final word. Today, many parents recoil from that approach—yet they're unsure what to say instead when their authority is challenged.

If *because I said so* feels too harsh, consider a modern equivalent:

Because it's the right thing to do.

This strikes a balance between authority and understanding. It conveys expectations while reinforcing moral reasoning and the concept of right and wrong. It also teaches children that not all decisions are up for debate, not because you're arbitrary, but because you're guiding them towards maturity and wisdom.

Parenting is a constant dance between understanding and leading, between empathy and authority. The balance is not easy, but it is essential.

A CALL TO PARENTAL MATURITY

Parenting invites us to embody the wisdom of seeking to understand rather than be understood. It's a call to step beyond our own need for validation and instead focus on understanding our children.

This does not mean surrendering authority or abandoning clear boundaries. Rather, it means recognising that true authority flows not from dominance but from love and understanding.

The paradox of parenting is that in seeking to understand our children, we often come to better understand ourselves. This is not an easy journey. It requires humility to listen, patience to guide, and courage to lead with clarity when needed. Yet, as we navigate this delicate dance between empathy and authority, between listening and leading, we model for our children the values we hope they will carry into their own lives.

By striving to understand our children, we teach them the value of connection and respect. By exercising loving authority, we show them the strength of guidance grounded in wisdom.

Parenting, then, becomes not just a role but a sacred calling—a channel through which peace and grace flow into your life and the lives of those around you.

In the end, parenting is an invitation to live out the wisdom of St. Francis's prayer—not to seek to be understood but to understand. When we embrace this, we don't just nurture our children's growth—we cultivate a relationship built on trust, wisdom, and love.

The world won't always explain itself, but our children will be better prepared to face it, with wisdom, resilience, and grace, carrying with them the quiet strength of having been truly understood.

12

Seek to Love Rather Than Be Loved

There is no doubt that being loved is one of the most wonderful experiences in the world. Love transforms, heals, and makes life's burdens more bearable. From the beginning, God recognised this truth: *It is not good for man to be alone* (Gen 2:18).

In Hebrew, the phrase used is *ezer kenegdo*, often translated as *helper*. It may sound modest, but its implications are profound. A strong marriage is more than mutual assistance; it is a sacred union reflecting God's design. If you've experienced a marriage where your spouse truly supports you, especially in the hard work of raising children, you know the beauty of this divine plan. And if you haven't, you know from its absence how essential that kind of love really is.

For those in 12-step recovery, the idea of love as a guiding principle will feel familiar. A Higher Power—however we understand it—is often described as a source of unconditional love that calls us to grow in love and service. Whether you call this force God, the Universe, or something else, the essence remains: love is transformative.

But the call to love extends far beyond marriage or family. Whether single or married, with children or without, we are all summoned to a life of love. Scripture is replete with commands about love:

- *Love one another as I have loved you* (John 13:34)
- *Love your neighbour as yourself* (Mark 12:31)
- *Love the Lord your God* (Mark 12:30)
- *Love your enemies* (Luke 6:35)

These verses leave no doubt that love is at the very heart of the Christian life. To be a follower of Jesus is to embrace love as both a calling and an identity. And while these commands are rooted in Christian scripture, the call to live a life of love transcends religious boundaries—it echoes across many spiritual paths as a sign of true growth and deep inner transformation.

THE CONSEQUENCES OF UNMET EMOTIONAL NEEDS

Sadly, examples abound of parents—Christian or otherwise—who fail to embody love even moderately well. Tragically, this has real and devastating consequences for their children, who grow up without a proper sense of being loved. This is not only a grave injustice but also a desperate societal problem.

Parents play an essential role in instilling a sense of worth and love in their children. This foundational experience enables those children to share love freely as they grow. When parents fail to provide sufficient love, children often become emotionally stunted, stuck in an unfulfilled need to be loved. This can lead to an inability to love others well, which is a profound tragedy. Love is paradoxical: when we give it freely, we receive it in return.

One of the most poignant illustrations of this dynamic came from a conversation I had with a mother taking one of my parenting courses. She was convinced her six-year-old daughter didn't love her. My heart broke for this child I had never met. The mother described her daughter squirming during hugs, turning away from kisses, and resisting affection. Eventually, she stopped trying altogether.

It sounded to me like a disorganised attachment—where a child both seeks and resists connection, often born of confusion, not rejection. I briefly considered whether autism or sensory issues might explain it, but that didn't seem to fit.

What I saw instead was a mother, poorly loved herself, who had developed a painful fixation on being loved by her child. She seemed to believe it was her daughter's role to offer unconditional affection and cooperation. This focus blinded her to the child's own emotional needs.

Beneath her anger, I sensed deep pain. Her daughter had inadvertently triggered old wounds, and she was holding the child responsible for them. Though she met her daughter's material needs, she was neglecting her emotional ones. Their relationship, fraught with misunderstanding, was becoming toxic.

This dynamic is not uncommon. Many parents assume that children possess an almost miraculous capacity to love their parents unconditionally, no matter what. And while it's true that most children do, at some deep level, love their parents, that love is not immune to damage. It can be obscured, sometimes deeply, by repeated hurts and unmet emotional needs.

Over time, this buried pain may harden into contempt, defiance, or even hatred. Yet even then, I see it as a kind of twisted love, distorted by disappointment. After all, one does not hate something or someone that one doesn't care about. Indifference, not hatred, is the truer opposite of love.

That's why I find it more troubling when a parent falls into indifference. While it's not unheard of for a parent to express open hostility towards their child, what is perhaps more common—and what can be just as devastating—is emotional neglect: a lack of warmth, empathy or interest. In many of these cases, the parent is not being deliberately cruel. They are simply unable to love well. Their own emotional wounds run deep, and their capacity for connection has been dulled or damaged by past trauma. Witnessing this is profoundly sorrowful, because the child suffers not from what is done, but from what is missing.

History offers many examples of broken parent–child relationships, but few are as tragic as that of King George II and his son, Prince Frederick of Wales. Their estrangement ran so deep that when Frederick's first child was born, he deliberately ensured his parents were not present, defying royal protocol. In the culture of the time, this was not just a family slight—it was a public insult. The Queen was furious and referred to her newborn granddaughter as a "poor ugly little she-mouse", a bitter comment that only widened the gulf. Years later, when Queen Caroline lay on her deathbed, Frederick wished to reconcile. But King George, still unyielding, refused to allow it.

No one came out of this well. A child was born into bitterness, a son postponed peace until it was too late, and a dying mother held her ground to the end. The whole saga is a case study in what happens when love is withheld and wounded pride is allowed to fester.

THE IDEAL AND THE REAL IN PARENTAL LOVE

Two myths persist in our cultural imagination—first, that parents (especially mothers) love unconditionally, and second, that women are inherently more loving than men. Both are comforting but misleading. Each contains a kernel of truth. But both are, ultimately, untrue.

Human beings—male and female—are not capable of perfect love. Only God loves that way. Even the most devoted parents are flawed and limited. Some come closer to the ideal than others, but none of us loves perfectly—not even our own children.

This truth should humble us. It reminds us that we must draw upon something greater than ourselves. Only by plugging into God's infinite love can we hope to love well, especially when stretched beyond our emotional limits.

Today, we often romanticise women as the more peaceful, loving sex. But women are just as affected by sin and woundedness as men. In 12-step recovery, I've heard countless stories from men and women raised by mothers whose ability to love was severely impaired, often due to trauma or addiction. These stories challenge the myth of maternal love as automatic or inevitable. The Christian understanding of the Fall offers clarity here: it is not a problem of gender—it is the human condition.

Women, too, are vulnerable to jealousy, resentment, and fear. When these wounds go unexamined, they can create a desperate need to be loved, one that may eclipse the capacity to love. Tragically, even children may be cast as emotional villains, blamed for failing to soothe a mother's inner pain.

To deny or downplay the reality of parental harm, especially maternal harm, is to dishonour the stories of children who have suffered. It adds insult to injury by leaving them unseen, unheard, and unvalidated. If we truly care about protecting and healing children, we must be willing to tell the truth, even when it's uncomfortable.

This is not about condemning mothers or parents in general. I write this not to shame but to free. We cannot grow as parents if we refuse to acknowledge our limitations. And we cannot love our children better if we cling to the flattering but false belief that we already love them perfectly.

A third myth, perhaps the most seductive of all, is that love comes naturally—that it's easy. But the evidence tells a different story. It's easy to fall in love. It's easier still to love people who meet our needs, or who love us back. But the kind of love that changes lives—the kind that is patient, sacrificial, and enduring—is hard. It demands practice, humility, and grace. It is not a feeling but a choice, made over and over again.

To love in the face of exhaustion, frustration, or conflict—to love all people at all times—is a nearly impossible standard. In fact, I doubt anyone has ever achieved it fully, apart from Mary, the mother of Jesus. In Catholic teaching, Mary is uniquely graced by God, making her an example of perfect human love. While not all Christian traditions share this understanding, it is a deeply held belief within the Catholic faith and a source of hope for those who look to her as a model of grace.

As both a psychologist and a mother, I have found this teaching about Mary intuitively and intellectually satisfying. Psychology underscores the vital role of love in the parent-child relationship, and from this perspective, it makes perfect sense that God would provide Mary with the extraordinary grace needed for such a vital role. As a mother, it is easy to see that raising a child, even in ordinary circumstances, is a deeply challenging task. Surely, it follows that for Mary to raise the son of God, who was both fully human and fully divine, God would grant her the fullness of his love and support to meet this sacred responsibility. Any parent can appreciate how profoundly fitting it is that she would be uniquely equipped for this role.

THE ONGOING CHALLENGE OF LEARNING TO LOVE

Having acknowledged the ways in which love can falter, particularly in the sacred task of parenting, it's clear that loving well is neither automatic nor easy. But failure in love is not the end of the story. Rather, it is a call to growth and to seek strength from a source greater than ourselves. For many, this is God, who offers infinite and unconditional love. For others, this power might come from the Universe, from being in nature, or from a deep sense of connection to something beyond the self. Wherever we find it, learning to love requires effort, discipline, and a willingness to draw on this spiritual sustenance in every moment.

This is not passive work. Across spiritual traditions, we are given tools to practise loving deliberately. In the Buddhist tradition, the Loving Kindness meditation begins with the simple prayer: *May all beings be free from suffering.* The practice extends compassion outward, even towards those who have hurt us. In 12-step recovery, there is a similarly radical suggestion: if you're resentful towards someone, pray for them daily for two weeks. Pray that they receive the things you wish for yourself—peace, freedom, joy. It's astonishing how often this softens the heart, not by minimising the harm, but by transforming the one doing the praying.

Practices like these take work. It's not easy to *pray for those who hurt you* (Matt 5:44). At first, it might even seem impossible. But if you're willing to try—and you practise it enough—it can become reflexive. If you don't, you'll remain stuck in the more natural reaction of hurting those who have hurt you. Revenge comes far more easily than forgiveness. If you doubt this, I refer you to the history of the human race.

The Christian command to *Love one another as I have loved you* (John 13:34) presents a radical challenge. It calls us to a revolutionary love that turns the other cheek and seeks the good even of our enemies. It's no wonder this message turned the world upside down. And yet, two thousand years later, we often behave as though we can love unconditionally without really trying. I prefer the idea that we must learn how to love.

It's a truth that resonates well beyond religion, finding its way into art, music, and culture. Consider the closing line of Eden Ahbez's song *Nature Boy*, made famous by Nat King Cole: "The greatest thing you'll ever learn is just to love and be loved in return." The sentiment captures something universal—an ache and a longing—that echoes in countless creative works, including Baz Luhrmann's *Moulin Rouge*, where the entire storyline revolves around that very idea.

Anyone who has ever fallen in love knows how wonderful it feels. At the start of a relationship, love seems effortless. But what is so special about this stage? Some theorists point to the collapse of ego boundaries, while others highlight the role of projection—we don't love the person as they truly are, but as we imagine them to be. Whatever the explanation, one thing is certain: this stage doesn't last.

When the first flush of new love fades, the real work of love begins. It's the same with parenting. Loving a baby comes easily, especially when that sweet baby is smiling up at us. The real challenge begins when that baby becomes a toddler, asserting his will and shattering the illusion of unconditional love. Loving well demands perseverance and, above all, sustenance—whether through faith, nature, or some other source of renewal that connects us to the bigger picture.

This is why the exhortations of saints to love until it hurts and then to love some more are so powerful. St Teresa of Calcutta, in particular, is well known for calling us to this radical level of self-sacrificial love.

However, I have come to see that love without truth is incomplete. The command to love our neighbour must always be understood in light of the command not to bear false witness. Authentic love is not only generous but also truthful.

LOVE IS WILLING THE GOOD OF THE OTHER

On the one hand, we are called to love with radical selflessness. On the other hand, we are called to be honest in that love. Here is another uncomfortable truth: we can only love as much as we are truly able. If we push ourselves too far beyond that capacity, it is no longer love—it becomes something else, like fear, resentment, or self-interest. Actions driven by these emotions can never have the same effect as those undertaken from a place of pure-hearted love.

This is why it is so important to know our limits and work to expand them gradually, but not recklessly. Loving well requires honesty, not just with others but also with ourselves.

Somewhat counterintuitively, one of the most helpful rules I've found for expanding my capacity to love is this: do not act out of resentment. Resentment is not necessarily a bad emotion—it often serves as a signal that a boundary has been crossed or a need has gone unmet. However, resentment becomes harmful if it festers, leading to bitterness or vindictiveness. When used wisely, it can guide us towards recognising where boundaries need to be set and maintained.

For example, as a mother, I often tried to be patient and forbearing with my children. But if I were not careful, I could push myself past the point of gracious forbearance into angry resentment. And acting from resentment never makes the world a better place. How could it? Love cannot thrive in a place of bitterness.

To give a concrete example, if I noticed I started to feel resentful at the thought of tidying up after my children, I knew it was time to take a different approach. Instead of tidying a bedroom or playroom myself, I might leave a note asking them to tidy up or make a verbal request for them to do so. Often, I gave a direct order, complete with a clear time frame. And on very rare occasions, when other strategies had failed, I was known to have rounded up the items scattered on the floor, placed them in a bin bag, and either put the bag in the attic, donated it to a charity shop, or—more drastically—thrown it away.

This approach may sound harsh, but the intention behind it is crucial. St Thomas Aquinas defined love as *willing the good of the other, as other*. From this perspective, teaching my children to respect their mother, to tidy up after themselves, and to do as they are asked by a legitimate authority figure, is an act of love. If I had given in to their moaning and resistance, and cleaned up myself, I would not be willing the good of my children. It is not good for them to feel entitled to have someone else tidy up for them. It is also an act of love for my children's future partners or spouses, who will benefit from them learning personal responsibility now.

The point of a parenting strategy like this is to act from love, not resentment or vindictiveness. If I act out of love, the result will be positive. There may be wailing and gnashing of teeth in the short term, but in the long term, such loving discipline bears fruit. Ideally, it encourages tidier habits, but more importantly, it fosters a deeper respect for the rules and for one's mother.

This principle is beautifully captured in scripture: *No discipline seems pleasant at the time; instead, it appears painful at best. Later on, however, it produces a harvest of righteousness and peace for those who have been trained by it* (Hebrews 12:11). I have tested this scripture countless times in my family, and I can vouch for its truthfulness. The unpleasantness of disciplining our children might make us want to shirk the responsibility, but I've found that taking a deep breath and proceeding with loving discipline is almost always the wiser choice.

As I write this, we are nearing the very end of the teenage years in our house. These years are often dreaded by parents, but in our family, they have been a time of unexpected joy. While we still faced plenty of dilemmas, I can say with gratitude that our teenagers became easier and more delightful as they matured. Loving discipline, grounded in clear intentions, has been one of the cornerstones of this surprising peace.

THE ROLE OF PRAYER IN EXPANDING LOVE

Balancing the practice of avoiding resentment with ceaseless prayers to become more loving is vital. I make it a priority to pray for the grace to love my family better. Without accompanying the practice of avoiding resentment with active efforts to expand our capacity to love, we risk falling into a subtle form of selfishness.

One of my favourite prayers for this purpose is the same one I quoted in the Prologue, borrowed from the song *Hosanna,* composed by Brooke Fraser (now Brooke Ligertwood): "Show me how to love like You have loved me." If we are commanded to love one another as Jesus has loved us, then it seems essential to pray for guidance in doing so. I used to favour listening to the music of Hillsong at very loud volumes while ironing as a form of prayer. It often moved me to tears, but I am also sure it expanded my heart. My shrivelled heart could not have grown without many bouts of such heartfelt praise and repentance.

As St. John of the Cross so wisely put it, "Where there is not love, put love, and there you will draw out love." This isn't just spiritual poetry—it's practical parenting advice. His simple yet profound teaching reminds us that our capacity for love can grow when we actively choose to act lovingly, even when we don't feel it initially. Prayer is one of the ways we put love into situations where it may feel absent, inviting divine grace to transform our hearts.

LOVE IN THE BALANCE

Another early lesson in expanding my capacity to love came when my daughter was a toddler, and her bedtime routine became a nightly exercise in stretching my boundaries. By then, I had the blessing of sobriety and no longer felt the pull of *wine-o'clock*, but I was torn between two parenting philosophies.

On one side were the pragmatic, behaviourist-oriented parents, who worried that staying with a child until they fell asleep prevented them from learning the essential skill of self-soothing. Their approach seemed more about suiting the parents' capacity than the child's needs, and it felt cold to me, rigid in its prioritisation of predictability and consistency. While these are important concepts, they are not panaceas and can risk leading to an unloving outcome.

On the other side were the attachment-oriented parents, who seemed to believe that a child required near-constant closeness and accommodation. While I valued strong attachment, I didn't believe a parent should indefinitely set aside her own needs for the child's sake. I simply couldn't get on board with the tendency towards parental martyrdom that often accompanied this approach. I also questioned the apparent belief in a child's inability to cope with small, everyday challenges, like going to bed, and the hesitation to trust in a child's capacity for resilience. The truth, as I discovered, lay somewhere in the balance.

My daughter's bedtime routine became a blend of both approaches. Most nights, I stayed with her until she drifted off, singing softly or telling stories. But some nights, when it was true, I explained that I needed to leave before she fell asleep and trusted that she would be okay. Usually, this was so I could attend a 12-step meeting or get needed time alone with my husband. While the routine often took 30 to 90 minutes—a significant sacrifice—it was ultimately worth it. My daughter became more secure, and I became more patient.

COMPETING MOTIVES

Over time, I've come to see that love and selfishness often coexist within us, pulling in opposite directions. Rarely are our motives pure. But recognising that doesn't mean we give up—it just means we need to become more intentional. One practice that's helped me is surprisingly simple: assigning percentages to my motives before I act. It sounds a bit odd, but it helps me check whether love is truly leading the way, or whether convenience, irritation, or ego is quietly in charge.

If my children seem genuinely tired earlier than usual, I might consider moving bedtime forward. But before doing so, I ask myself: *Am I doing this mostly for them, or mostly because I want to be done for the day?* If I sense that at least 60% of my intention is genuinely about their well-being, I go ahead. If the larger motive is my own impatience, I'll stick to the usual routine.

Or take a more adult example: if I'm tempted to correct my husband for leaving the back door unlocked, I'll pause to reflect. If I'm mostly motivated by care for our safety—say, 60% or more—I'll speak up. But if I realise that what's really bubbling up is criticism or irritation, I'll hold off until I can come at it with more love and less blame.

This habit has helped me love more intentionally. It doesn't mean I always get it right, but it has made me more mindful of how mixed motives can shape the tone and outcome of my interventions. This little tool has helped me put love into situations where it might otherwise have been missing.

LOVE AS THE CORNERSTONE OF PARENTING

None of us gets it right all the time. Our motives are mixed, our energy limited. But love can grow if we commit to learning.

Parenting offers countless opportunities to grow in love, but it also exposes our limitations. Through prayer, reflection, and daily practice, I have learned that my capacity to love, though far from perfect, can expand. The role of the parent is to love their child, and loving well means constantly striving to act with pure intentions.

Ultimately, when we act out of love, we make the world a better place. By focusing on loving others rather than seeking love for ourselves, we often find that love returns to us in abundance.

As our children transition into young adulthood, I find myself deeply grateful for the joy these years have brought and for the lessons learned along the way. Though challenges were inevitable, the peace that came from love and intentional discipline has helped us through even the hardest moments. Watching our teenagers mature into delightful and competent young adults has been one of the greatest rewards of this journey.

When we commit to becoming channels of peace in our families, rooted in love, honesty, and grace, we fulfil the spirit of St. Francis's prayer. Where there is no love, we can choose to put love. And there, we will draw out love—not just in our families, but in the world around us.

13

It Is in Self-Forgetting That One Finds

'.....what did he mean by self-forgetting, and how did he propose to accomplish that?.....'

—The Twelve Steps and Twelve Traditions, p.101

Let's clear up a common misconception first: *forgetting oneself* and *losing oneself* are not interchangeable. They are not the same thing at all, not even close. Losing one's mind, especially, is definitely not self-forgetting. I should know because I almost lost mine.

Long before my spiritual awakening, I was aware of the Eastern concept of the self as an illusion and a source of suffering, aware that non-attachment to the self was desirable. I was also aware of psycho-philosophical ideas of the self as constructed by the mind as a function of the brain.

I practised becoming detached from myself by various means, such as meditation and autogenic training, and owning a copy of *The Tibetan Book of the Dead*. In truth, I was as frightened by the prospect of losing my sense of self at the point of death as I was by the Christian concepts of purgatory and hell.

The promise of reincarnation as a mindful being who could remember past lives was intoxicating. The idea that I would miss out on such a prize through my own failure to master myself in this life, and particularly in death, was anxiety-inducing, to say the least. By the way, I am not claiming that my understanding of Tibetan Buddhism is correct; I am merely saying that this is how I understood it in my late teens and twenties.

I understood that a mindful death, made possible by attaining enlightenment during this life, would lead to the possibility of either a) choosing to merge with the Cosmic Force, which would result in the loss of my selfhood as a human being (which sounded alternately like the perfect solution to my suffering or like the most horrendous loss I could imagine). Or alternatively, b) choosing to reincarnate on earth as an enlightened being in order to help others attain enlightenment, like the Dalai Lama. This appealed to both my loving nature, which desired to help others, and my ego, which desired to be powerful and important.

But both these options required enlightenment in this life, and if I didn't attain that, then it would be option c) being condemned to reincarnate again and start all over from scratch. This puzzle kept me awake for months, and I became so miserable that losing consciousness forever by merging with the Divine or the Universe or whatever it was sounded like a perfect solution.

THE CONVENIENCE OF ESCAPE

Despite the conundrum, the thought of leaving behind all my loved ones sounded dreadful. Was this just because I was unhelpfully attached to them? But this merging would only be possible if I'd attained enlightenment, which seemed unlikely given how attached I was to certain things. Besides, I'd had the misfortune to be born in Ireland rather than Tibet, so I was already twenty years behind schedule. I had a lot of catching up to do.

But I wasn't even sure I wanted the prize. All this ruminating about whether I fancied self-annihilation by merging with the Divine or reincarnation, whether by default or design, ultimately did nothing to make me forget about myself. In fact, it kept me as self-centred and trapped as ever. I didn't realise it at the time, but there is a big difference between Eastern detachment from the self and self-forgetting, as the St. Francis prayer means it.

Another dead-end worth mentioning, and I speak from personal experience, is that you will not forget yourself or find yourself by the use of alcohol and drugs. Nonetheless, this does not stop both remaining popular methods in the quest to find oneself. As one loses touch with a great proportion of one's mind when indulging in such substances, and as the mind is often mistaken for the self, it isn't too mysterious that people try to forget themselves this way. Alas, the drugs and alcohol always wear off. Then, the self is back, usually with a vengeance.

The gap year (or years) phenomenon is another popular modern method to find oneself. Perennially popular with young adults, older adults try it, too. Perhaps, like me, you find it hard to believe that grown-ups leave marriages and jobs, sometimes even their children, to go find themselves.

Eat Pray Love, Elizabeth Gilbert's story of leaving her marriage to embark on a journey of self-discovery, became a worldwide phenomenon. While I very much enjoyed her story of being sent back to bed by the voice of God, I engaged in a fair bit of eye-rolling through the rest of the book. *How is this not selfishness personified,* I wondered? *She walked away from her marital vows because she was bored?*

She left her husband and swapped her already privileged life for the further privilege of a yearlong sabbatical in Italy, India, and

Bali. Was I supposed to admire this? To believe it was courageous and necessary? I clearly recall thinking: *I'm not buying it*. Then, as now, I think walking out of your marriage in the absence of abuse is bad behaviour. I also noted that God told her to go back to bed, but going to India? That, I suspected, was her own idea.

These methods are destined to fail because they put the cart before the horse. They prioritise the finding part rather than the forgetting part. The prayer of St. Francis is all about this distinction. If you want to be forgiven, forgive. If you want to be loved, love. And if you want to find yourself, you've got to forget yourself. Or better yet, find others. You'll be so busy serving them, you'll forget yourself without even trying. When people set off to find themselves, they are skipping over the first, more important part of the equation.

CREATING ONE LIFE WHERE THERE HAD BEEN TWO

Eventually, I outgrew this concern about finding myself and became preoccupied with self-improvement instead. This, unsurprisingly, was during the stage of affirmations and education when I focused on getting one degree after another.

It was an enjoyable time in many ways. I met my husband around the same time, and we set about finding ourselves in achievement, materialism, and each other. My marriage hinted at the extent of my selfishness since it was not easy for me and my husband to create one life where there had been two.

It took quite a while for us to learn how to prioritise each other rather than our families of origin. Thankfully, we managed it just enough to avoid separation or divorce. But we were still tragically selfish, and we caused each other a lot of pain. Eventually, I got out of this cul-de-sac and was set on the right path.

I met some people who really helped me with this self-forgetting business. They told me my biggest problem was pride, which they defined as self-centred fear and selfishness. My alternately exalted and debased sense of self was causing a lot of trouble, they said. I was an egomaniac with a chip on my shoulder, and the antidote to these problems was humility. I had absolutely forgotten that in Christian doctrine, pride is the cardinal sin, and humility is the virtue that combats it. I decided to investigate this theory.

It is unedifying to have to admit it, but I was arrogant enough to believe that the result of my investigation might be other than agreement. Fortunately for me, I discovered they were right and became willing to practice this humility thing I so poorly understood, but it wasn't an easy endeavour.

THE PERILS OF PRIDE

I am naturally disposed to be prideful. It is easy for me to believe that I am *more* than others, more kind, more generous, more deserving, more of anything, really. The flip side to this coin is that I can also easily believe that I am *less* than others, less important, less interesting, less worthy.

Despite being prideful, I suffered in the past from tragically poor self-esteem, as well as virtually non-existent self-worth. In Christian thinking, these are all just manifestations of the same problem— pride. Pride causes you to believe that you are either better or worse than others.

At the heart of pride, I was told, is fear. Fear of what people think of me, for example. I needed to stop worrying so much about what people thought of me, which I was told was being self-centred. Furthermore, I was generally spending too much time thinking about myself. I would be a lot happier, not to mention more useful, if I stopped thinking about myself so much, and after some thought, this rang true. Neuroscience seems to agree: thinking about yourself is neurologically indistinguishable from being miserable, anxious, or depressed. In other words, self-centredness really does make you suffer.*

Be Self Aware, Not Self Obsessed

I used to spend an inordinate amount of time thinking about myself. In fact, I used to worry that there was something wrong with me because I spent so much time thinking about myself. My thoughts about myself ranged over what was happening in my present, what might happen in my future, and especially, what had happened in my past. I was particularly good at rehearsing past grievances. I was at the mercy of self-piteous thoughts and regrets, and I particularly regretted a past that had *never existed*.

This problem had been in place for a long time. I remember being dismayed *as a teenager* about how frequently I seemed to think of myself. I found it tedious and embarrassing, yet I didn't seem able to stop. Despite the boring nature of having the same thoughts over and over, as the material of my life was, as yet, rather limited, I actually found myself fascinated.

* This idea is supported by neuroscience research showing that excessive self-focused thinking is linked to increased activity in the brain's Default Mode Network, which has been associated with depression and anxiety. See *"The Neuroscience of Mind-Wandering,"* Scientific American, 2014.

When I wasn't thinking about myself, I wondered what other people thought of me. I remember musing about whether they could tell how frequently I was thinking of myself. This sort of thinking demonstrates how a self-centred soul can manage to think of another person, but really only in relation to themselves.

I'm reminded of the joke about the person who, having spent an hour speaking non-stop about himself to his lunch companion, finally pauses and says, "Enough about me. What do YOU think of me?" I assume from the existence of this joke that I am not the only human being to have wrestled with such a degree of self-centredness. It led me to really ponder the true meaning of humility.

Humility is not thinking less of yourself; it is thinking of yourself less. I love this definition of humility because you will notice that thinking of yourself less is a reasonable definition of self-forgetting.

THE FREEDOM OF MAKING AMENDS

The other important way to practice self-forgetting, I was taught in recovery, was that I must become willing to make amends for my mistakes, my errors, my bad behaviour, and my lapses in love. It was presupposed that I would harm people with my pride and other defects of character. Imagine that!

Well, when you have poor self-worth, it is acutely painful to admit your faults, but I did it. And weirdly, by doing it, I began to develop self-worth and self-esteem. I developed self-esteem because esteem comes from doing estimable things.

Admitting you've done wrong and apologising to the person you have wronged is an estimable act. Vowing not to behave like that again and then following through is another. These same behaviours helped me develop self-worth, because when you have sufficient humility to admit you've been in the wrong or made a mistake, it brings you closer to God. And when that happens, you can't help but feel better about yourself.

If all this sounds like a confession, then you're right—it is. Being in recovery brought me back to the practice of confession: *Confess your sins to each other and pray for one another so that you might be healed* (James 5:16).

Teaching my children about the need to make amends for their behaviour when they have done wrong has been of great benefit to our family. It's a two-way street, of course, and I have learned to apologise to them for my wrongdoings, seek their forgiveness, and—this is vital—undertake with fervour to rid myself of whatever defect drove the behaviour I needed to make amends for.

I would not have had the first idea of how to handle all sorts of situations had I not become acquainted with the concept of making amends through recovery. I consider it one of God's greatest favours for me. He has helped me to break these chains from my birth family, where we never apologised for anything. With my husband and children, we do our best to quickly admit when we are wrong and not let the sun go down on a fight. This wasn't easy at first. But we got there eventually. Most of the time.

I can vouch for the fact that life is far more enjoyable since I have been somewhat relieved of the bondage of self. I've stopped worrying so much about what other people think of me, and as a result, I've found greater peace.

RISE BY LIFTING OTHERS

Here's another sure-fire way to forget about yourself: service to others. This is an excellent method for self-forgetting, though it has fallen into disrepute these days, as one keeps oneself *safe* and prioritises *self-care*. Service to others is at the core of the Christian path for transformation. If done properly, this will serve to shrink our egos and reduce our selfishness. As an added bonus, it is beneficial for the person we serve, too.

Another way to say that you'll find yourself through self-forgetting is to say you'll find yourself through love, because *to love is to extend yourself for the good of the other*. To love is to choose the other person over yourself, to serve them, not yourself.

By necessity, this means forgetting about yourself. That's why I say it needs to be done properly, since I have found that it is possible to serve others out of a self-aggrandising motive. Serving others can actually *grow* the ego rather than shrink it. A fact that is sad but true.

Marriage, Parenthood and the Road to Selflessness

Personally, I have found that marriage and motherhood are rather effective vehicles for self-forgetting, as you cannot be a wife or mother without much service to others. I had a rude awakening about how selfish I still was when I became a mother. Responding to another human being's needs, regardless of what was going on with me, was insanely difficult. I figured out it was hard because I was still selfish and self-centred despite three years of marriage.

For instance, I might find it easy to respond to my infant firstborn son, but doing that while retaining my good humour and not falling out with my husband about how much and exactly what he was doing to help was profoundly difficult. It stands to reason that selfishness had taken serious root in my heart by the time I had my first child, aged thirty-one.

I had spent almost my whole life up to that point nurturing selfishness. I didn't realise this, of course—I thought I was a reasonably non-selfish person. But that turned out to be a delusion. Even though my marriage had considerably reduced my selfishness because I had learned to (sometimes) put my husband's needs and desires ahead of my own. Still, I was a master of resentful giving. And I was shocked to discover that serving my baby son was, in some ways, even more onerous than serving my husband.

If I were the inventive type, I'd love to invent a machine that could tell you what percentage of your day was spent in which emotions. So, for example, at the end of the day, you'd get a printout showing: joy 13%, anger 27%, fear 38%, sadness 21%, surprise 1%. Even better, I wish we could find a way to quantify self-centredness: the percentage of actions today motivated by concern for self (81%) and concern for others (19%). I'd want this machine because I'd love to know how my progress towards being a less self-centred person is really going, rather than having to rely on my own (very unreliable) sense of how it's going.

One day soon, we may be able to simply electrically stimulate part of our brains in order to eradicate feelings of uselessness and self-pity. We might learn how to erase shame or turn off anger. It could be possible that we'll be able to forget ourselves by stimulating just the right part of the brain, finally being relieved of the bondage of self, not through surrender, but through science.

Until that day arrives, however, and in case it just turns out to be another version of spiritual bypass, I think I'll keep following this path to self-forgetting that I have been on. Like millions of people before me, I have discovered that I like myself better when I think about myself less and serve others more. In self-forgetting, I have found.

14

It Is in Forgiving That We Are Forgiven

Growing up in a Christian world, you cannot avoid the word forgiveness. If you're raised in a denomination that says the Lord's Prayer, you will find yourself reciting it *as we forgive those who trespass against us* hundreds of times during childhood. For a Mass-going Catholic, it's a weekly ritual. In my junior school, we prayed after lunch every day, always including the Our Father. Each school morning began with at least one prayer—usually, you guessed it, the Our Father.

I have vivid memories of girls fainting during morning prayers in the third class. Our teacher that year, let's call her Mrs Boyle, kept us standing for what felt like an eternity, rattling off prayer after prayer. Coming in from the frosty Irish mornings to a warm classroom didn't help. Fainting, vomiting, and toileting accidents became almost routine—perhaps our young bodies were protesting the only way they knew how. Even so, one thing stood out: the idea of forgiveness was everywhere, threaded through every recitation, every ritual.

But what were we meant to forgive? *Everything.* How often? *Always.* Any exceptions? *None.* Seriously? *Yes, seriously.* It was a daunting standard—one that seemed impossible to meet. God forgave us, so we were expected to forgive others. No matter how big or small the offence, or how much you might prefer to hold a grudge. Yet the *how-to* of forgiveness remained vague, buried beneath esoteric language about sanctification and grace, or abstract advice about becoming Christlike by keeping our eyes on Jesus.

As a child, I struggled to make sense of it all. What did eating a wafer at Mass have to do with forgiving my sister for taking my book? It was so hard for me to extract anything practical about the lived reality of forgiveness from this well-intentioned Catholic catechesis.

What does it mean, in practical terms, to let go of anger or resentment and forgive? How do we, as imperfect people, embrace the near-impossible standard of forgiving everything, always, with no exceptions? And how do we make this timeless concept relevant in a world so different from the one in which I stood, bored and confused, in Mrs Boyle's classroom?

CREATING ACCOUNTABILITY

There's so much emphasis these days on the seemingly lovely idea that human beings are intrinsically good. Even in the Christian schools my children attended, this notion was pervasive. On the surface, it sounds good, doesn't it? If everyone is inherently good, then there's no such thing as sin, and therefore nothing to forgive. But is this true? And even if it were, what does that mean for the hurts and wrongs we inevitably experience?

I've heard plenty of adults dismiss another person's upset with the casual logic of *That's their stuff.* It's easier to think the other person's reaction is the problem than to admit you've done something wrong, or, at the very least, offended them. The modern logic goes something like this: if I didn't mean to hurt you, then I haven't done anything wrong, and you shouldn't be upset. To this, I say: if a tree falls in the woods but didn't intend to, is it still on the ground? Of course, it is. The branches are broken, the grass is crushed, and the squirrel that called it home now needs a new one. Intention doesn't erase impact.

This kind of thinking also absolves me of the need for your forgiveness, of the need to apologise or change my behaviour. It's very convenient for my ego, which hates admitting I'm wrong. But it's devastating for relationships, which suffer or even cease when we refuse to acknowledge the hurt we've caused.

Then there's the popular idea that we're all doing the best we can. I've found this idea helpful, up to a point. Accepting that this applies to people who hurt me allowed me to let go of resentments I carried for years. But if taken to extremes, it becomes an excuse for bad behaviour: if everyone is doing their best, then no one is ever in the wrong, and forgiveness becomes unnecessary. This interpretation undermines accountability, and I'm convinced it is making true forgiveness harder, not easier.

This avoidance of accountability has crept into all areas of life, including parenting. Perhaps in the past, parents understood that forgiveness was part of the deal. These days, however, it's rarely mentioned. In the many secular parenting books and articles I've read, not once have I come across the idea that I'd need to forgive my children, again and again.

Some trespasses are minor: your toddler writes in crayon on the freshly painted living room walls—again, despite yesterday's warning. Others are more serious: your teenager gets arrested for underage drinking. And then there are the ones that blindside you entirely, like finding out your child has been living a double life online, posting things they'd never say at home, or hiding a relationship they knew you wouldn't allow. Each one challenges you to forgive—and keep forgiving.

Forgiving your child, over and over, isn't just an act of love; it's a practice of humility and accountability. It acknowledges their humanity and yours. And perhaps that's the point: forgiveness isn't about excusing wrongdoing but about creating space for growth, repair, and reconnection.

But accountability doesn't come naturally to any of us, especially when our ego gets in the way. The same ego that convinces us we're justified in our irritation or anger is often what prevents us from seeing the truth. It convinces us we shouldn't have to forgive; that the fault lies entirely with the other person; that admitting our own flaws would be too painful to bear.

This reluctance to face our ego's role in our relationships often leaves us stuck. We're busy trying to fix or control everything around us, but rarely do we pause to confront the ways our wounded pride, impatience, or desire for control might be causing harm. And nowhere is this more evident than in our relationships with our children.

It's here—at the messy intersection of love, responsibility, and ego—that things get especially tricky. Because when it comes to our children, we're not just parents—we're also people. And people, inevitably, get hurt.

Unmasking Your Ego

You see, that's the problem—or at least a large part of the problem. We're so busy trying to organise and manage the practicalities of our children's lives that we forget, if we ever even knew it in the first place, how important it is to forgive them when they've hurt us. In fact, we spend a lot of energy trying to pretend they don't hurt us, which is nonsense, of course. They do hurt us; it's inevitable.

We need to get better at acknowledging this before we end up sulking or screaming.

Instead of saying, *You've hurt me*, we prefer to say things like *I'm very disappointed in you*, or *That makes me so angry*, different iterations to hide what we actually mean. All the little hurts our children inflict on us are what's behind our tantrums and outbursts, and they're also behind the wounded silences we often inadvertently subject our children to.

My daughter was a few years old when I began to realise that I often had resentment towards her. When I sat down to explore the resentment in real time, I uncovered the fact that this was a theme for us. It was an unpleasant discovery.

I didn't like that I was the kind of person who would feel resentment towards my three-year-old daughter. But I held on to the belief that truth could set me free—truth about myself, even when it was uncomfortable to face. My faith teaches me that I am loved deeply, not because of my perfection, but despite my flaws. It asks me to trust that love is transformative, even when I struggle to see myself as deserving of it.

Who was I, then, in the midst of this mess? Who was this person that God had loved so completely, fought to redeem, and believed was worth saving? As I wrestled with these questions, I began to see that recognising my shortcomings wasn't meant to lead me to despair but to growth, healing, and freedom.

It turned out that answering those questions wasn't easy—or pretty. When I took an honest look at myself, I had to admit that I was far from perfect. I was, to borrow a phrase from my faith, a total sinner—the kind of mother who could get cross at her daughter multiple times a day but not say anything. Instead, I would store up all the irritation and hurt until my 6 pm meltdown. Then, all my pent-up frustration and resentment would come pouring out. My outburst would provide temporary relief but ultimately leave me feeling worse when my righteousness subsided, and the misery, shame, and guilt kicked in.

Setting Boundaries as an Act of Love

It was actually a relief when God decided to teach me about the need to regularly clear out the resentment that I found so easy to carry about my daughter. I learned that we usually end up in a place of hard feelings because I'd let her cross a boundary I didn't realise I had. Little by little, after a lot of prayer and contemplation, my boundaries became clearer to me, which was good because now they could be clearer to my children.

It would be years later that I finally discovered Dr Cloud's and Dr Townsend's book on boundaries, written from an explicitly Christian perspective. When I read the following sentence, I jotted it down because it resonated with me so profoundly: "The first thing necessary for raising a child with boundaries is a parent with boundaries."

The process of noticing when I felt resentful towards one of my children started to get me in touch with my limits. It turned out I was able to be a better version of myself when I wasn't letting other people walk all over me, no matter how little they were or whether they were related to me or not. I felt better about myself, and I liked my children better. I could act before irritation and anger got the better of me, and consequently, I had to forgive myself and my children less.

This is how it works in God's economy: when I acted as if I actually had limits to my ability to be tolerant and patient, I became more loving and patient. I shouted less and, as a result, fell into despair less. And that meant I behaved less like a person that my family members had to forgive. It was one of those things that made me marvel at how spiritual physics works and how God has orchestrated everything.

It amazes me to think that a viable solution to selfishness — and the inability to love without limits—is to acknowledge you have limits and not push yourself too far beyond them. Lo and behold, if you stick to this, you paradoxically become a person who can extend yourself further and further. Over time, your heart grows, and you find you are capable of doing things that you simply couldn't do before.

How does this work in practice? Here's a concrete example. I had to admit to myself that I was only a moderately patient person. I didn't have it in me to allow my children to ignore me when I called them for dinner. I was self-centred enough to require verbal acknowledgement that they were on their way to the table. And when we had gathered in the kitchen or dining room, and sat down for our meal together, then I wanted to hear "Thank you" for the food I'd prepared.

I often wished I could serve like Florence Nightingale, but I couldn't. If I let my children *not* do these things (come promptly when called; say thank you when served), then I was going to feel resentful. Sooner or later, that would come out sideways, and my children will bear the brunt of it.

Then, and this is the part that seems miraculous, by insisting that I be treated with respect, I somehow (by God's grace, I suppose) became a person who is less prone to resentment and more able to serve without limit.

In further silver linings, it turns out that it's better for a child, too, if his parent treats him like this. That child will find it easier to become a person who is considerate of other human beings and be grateful for his many blessings, like plenty of delicious, nutritious food that he didn't have to buy or prepare! How amazing is that?

I'm making a case in this chapter that we should learn how to forgive. I'm also making the case for becoming the kind of people who require less forgiveness from others. This is an act of love for the people around us, as well as beneficial for ourselves.

The benefit to self is obvious: you become a better version of yourself and a more peaceful person. However, by doing this, you also provide a great service to others: because it is tricky to forgive, you help others avoid the burden of carrying resentment towards you.

REASONS AREN'T EXCUSES

As we've seen, learning to forgive involves recognising our own limits and setting boundaries. But it also requires understanding that circumstances don't excuse behaviour—our children's or our own. Forgiveness doesn't mean pretending bad behaviour didn't happen, and it certainly doesn't mean tolerating it indefinitely. It's in your child's best interest to learn to behave like the kind of small person their own parents and other adults don't get easily annoyed with.

Adults today often pretend that all children are likeable. They're not. Poor behaviour makes a person dislikeable and in need of forgiveness, no matter their age. Of course, we might understand that troublesome behaviour stems from difficult circumstances, but that doesn't mean we're unaffected by it. There are reasons for *all* behaviour, good and bad. Just as having diligent, loving parents doesn't erase the positive effects of your good deeds, having neglectful or challenging parents doesn't erase the negative effects of bad ones.

I've encountered many parents who claim their children are desperately ungrateful. To cope with their irritation and despair about this, they often turn to other parents for validation. Their strategy? Venting through sarcasm-laden stories about their children's entitled behaviour.

In such moments of frustration, some parents funnel their negative feelings into humour that's laced with a tone that betrays their hurt. They say the kinds of things they wouldn't want their children to hear, or at least, they shouldn't. In some families, things may have deteriorated to the point where these stories are shared openly, even in front of the children. When that happens, the contempt is impossible to ignore, and the atmosphere is poisoned by hostility.

If open contempt between family members has become the order of the day, you can bet there's a mountain of hurt and resentment waiting to be forgiven.

The Lists That Set Us Free

If you can't name dozens—or at least a handful—of things you've *consciously* forgiven your child for, it's time to start practising. Forgiveness is a muscle, and it grows stronger with use. Start by writing a list of the resentments you hold towards your child.

If you think you don't have any, that's fine—but dig a little deeper. Write a list of all the times they annoyed you, hurt you, or made you despair that they'd ever turn out all right. Even small grievances count. You can keep it brief with bullet points or go into detail with paragraphs. If necessary, write pages. Whatever helps you get it out of your head and onto paper.

Once you've created your list, the next step is to explore why each thing bothers you. Does it make you feel unimportant, disrespected, or even invisible? Maybe it threatens your sense of financial security, your reputation, or your vision of how things should be. Does it wound your pride or self-esteem? The key is to figure out what's at the root of your irritation or hurt.

Now comes the hardest part: looking at your own role in the situation. What are you contributing to this resentment? What aspects of your character or behaviour might be playing a part? This isn't about blaming yourself but about taking an honest inventory of your weaknesses.

Ask yourself:

- Am I impatient or quick to anger?
- Do I struggle to let go of things?
- Am I prone to self-pity or despair?
- Do I exaggerate others' faults?
- Do I focus on others' mistakes while ignoring my own?

- Am I critical, sarcastic, or condescending in word or tone?
- Do I try to control or micromanage others?
- Do I expect my family members to read my mind instead of clearly stating my needs?
- Do I hide my feelings of upset or disappointment, hoping others will notice or guess?
- Am I unwilling to admit when I'm wrong?

The more you practise, the easier it will become to identify your part in these situations. This process isn't comfortable. But it's worth it. You'll begin to see yourself and your own flaws more clearly, and you may come to a deeper understanding of your need for forgiveness and grace, whether from a higher power, the people you've wronged, or even yourself.

For me, this practice of getting to know myself as I truly was also opened my eyes to something that had once seemed strange and even esoteric: the Christian idea that we need a saviour—that *Jesus died for my sins*. Like many people, I used to think this was self-flagellating medieval nonsense. But after years in 12-step recovery and becoming fluent in personal inventory, it started to make sense—to seem obviously true, even. Seeing my own flaws so clearly helped me understand just how universal this need for grace and redemption really is.

It is much harder to hold onto a grudge when you're faced with a written list of your own failings. What often happens is this: you might initially believe your child's behaviour fully justified your reaction. But when you take the time to ask *What am I doing that's contributing to this resentment*, you'll start to see that you've been playing a role in your own misery.

And that changes everything. It's much easier to forgive someone when you recognise that your own actions or attitudes may not have been perfect, either. From there, it's a smaller step to drop the rock of resentment, let go of the hurt, and embrace forgiveness.

The Space Forgiveness Creates

I knew a woman some years ago, a lovely young American lady who had found her way into recovery from alcoholism. When it came time for her to attempt Step 4 in the recovery process—making a searching and fearless moral inventory—her sponsor gave her some unexpected advice. Instead of simply putting her husband's name on the list of people she was resentful towards, the sponsor suggested she write down every individual resentment she held against him.

As you can imagine, this was a Herculean task. But my friend complied, pouring out every single resentment she could think of. It took courage and honesty, but she did it.

When she shared about this process years later, she described how transformative it was. Her sponsor had told her that by listing each specific resentment, she would gain freedom from every single one, and she found this wisdom to be true. Letting go of those individual grievances freed her from the weight of the hurt she had been carrying and allowed her to enjoy her marriage in a way she hadn't thought possible. The process transformed her relationship and helped her become the kind of wife she wanted to be.

Who wouldn't want that?

So, I encourage you to be brave. Try not to worry about the fact that the person you're writing about is your beloved child. Needing to forgive them doesn't diminish your love for them—it deepens it. Keep reminding yourself that the truth will set you free. The truth is that God already knows you fully and completely. He knows you're sometimes inclined to be a grudge-keeping, resentful, limited, impatient, jealous, fearful, human being. And yet, he loves you anyway.

But here's the thing: he also loves you far too much to leave you like that.

Forgiveness isn't just about what you let go of; it's about what you receive in return. When you face all your emotional baggage and release it to something greater than yourself, you make room for something better. For me, this has meant leaving it at the foot of his cross, trusting in God's grace to transform what I cannot fix on my own. But whatever your spiritual framework, the act of letting go creates space for freedom, for healing, and for the possibility of becoming the parent, spouse, or friend you truly want to be.

So get ready. Get ready to let go of the unforgiveness that's been weighing you down—the grievances, resentments, and pain you've been carrying. For me, this has meant leaving it at the foot of his cross, trusting in God's grace to transform what I cannot fix on my own. But wherever you find your power, the act of releasing these burdens creates space for freedom, for healing, and for discovering that it really is in forgiving that we are forgiven.

15

It Is in Giving That One Receives

Every parent encounters the truth of this great spiritual axiom in the earliest moments of their journey into parenthood. New parents may not consciously realise it at the time, but when we have a child, we invite this truth into our lives in the most profound sense possible.

The understanding of this concept is even enshrined in our language – the mother *gives* birth while the child *receives* life. And in giving the gift of life, the mother and father receive one of the greatest gifts imaginable. However, it is difficult to incorporate this wisdom in the long term. Inevitably, perhaps even daily, we reach the limits of our capacity to give, and when this happens, the results are usually not pretty.

I was struck one night by something I heard a facilitator on a marriage preparation course say: 'Whenever we are less than loving to our spouse, we cause harm'. It stuck in my mind because it seemed like an excessively high standard. *Really?* I thought.

Every time? Every single time we are less than loving, do we inevitably cause harm?

But even as I recoiled from the idea that I could harm my spouse so easily, and so unintentionally, I recognised the kernel of truth in what had been said. Real love—the kind that gives without holding back, that puts another first—is both beautiful and costly. We may not always realise it in the moment, but when we withhold love, we create a kind of deficit. A missed opportunity to give. And when that happens often enough, it adds up.

Most of us want to love generously, but we bump into our own limitations daily—fatigue, resentment, the need to be seen or appreciated. We're not bottomless wells. Giving without limit isn't something we can achieve through sheer willpower, and those rare people who seem able to do it are often the ones we quietly call saints. What they show us, though, is that this kind of self-giving isn't about striving—it's about grace. And grace, thankfully, doesn't require us to be flawless before it begins to flow.

THE STRUGGLES OF CONDITIONAL LOVE

It's one thing to admire the beauty of selfless love in theory—quite another to practice it in a kitchen with a stubborn six-year-old.

I remember getting my mental knickers in a twist when I found myself telling my daughter that if she wouldn't cooperate with me, then I was disinclined to cooperate with her. The incident melted my head because I could tell I was demonstrating and, therefore, teaching, conditional love. But at the same time, I was telling the truth.

In that moment, I hit the edge of my ability to give. The wisdom that I would receive if only I could give was lost to me entirely. Worse still, I was aware of a subtle motive behind my words—a hope that she might be shamed or nudged into cooperation. *Was this gentle manipulation? Or was it a mother lovingly teaching her child a hard truth about how the world really works?*

I had seen what happened when people gave and gave, but couldn't or wouldn't receive: they didn't become beacons of love—they became doormats. Resentful ones. And often, instead of raising up the people they were trying to serve, they seemed to diminish them. Endless giving without joy doesn't just hollow out the giver; it also starves the receiver of the opportunity to grow into someone capable of giving in return.

If your generosity leads someone to become selfish rather than grateful, is it really love? I don't think so. You can tell a tree by its fruit, after all (Matt 12:33)—and you can't gather figs from hawthorns (Luke 6:44).

Maybe this is why some children seem so ungrateful, even when they've been given everything. Have the parents wandered beyond their true capacity to give, and found themselves bitter and bewildered by the results? Giving from a place of resentment won't bring about the same fruit as giving from a place of love.

Is giving tainted with resentment really giving at all? Well, it depends on who you ask. The giver of this kind of reluctant bestowing tends to say yes. They did the thing. But the receiver may feel something else entirely.

Think of all the people in the world who will not ask for help, even when they're in real need. People who squirm when they receive a compliment, deflect a kindness, or feel embarrassed by a gift. What are they picking up on? Maybe it's a sense of obligation. Or judgement. Or the unspoken price tag that so often clings to help that isn't freely given.

There's a reason some of us find it hard to receive. We've been on the other end of a kind of giving that didn't feel like love—it felt like control, or pity, or martyrdom. And once you've experienced that kind of giving, it changes you. You learn to duck. You learn to pretend you don't need anything. You learn that it's safer not to receive at all.

The Power and Limits of Generosity

The notion that untainted giving can turn a life around runs deep in the human psyche. The moment of pure grace when one limited human being gives to another can be life-changing.

We see this kind of life-changing, grace-infused generosity in Victor Hugo's *Les Misérables*, a deeply Christian story of redemption brought about by an act of unmerited compassion. The human soul is moved by such grace, not only when we receive it ourselves, but even when we merely witness it. It touches something deep within us.

And yet, it doesn't always work like that.

Even heroic generosity doesn't always help someone stay on track. There are plenty of examples where a parent gives selflessly, and yet the child does not turn their life around. Love doesn't always seem to work—at least not in the way we hope.

What if it really is as simple as Jesus implies when he says we will know a tree by its fruit? If a good tree cannot produce bad fruit, then what are we to make of children who fall far short of their parents' apparent goodness?

We are on dangerous ground here. There are more influences on a child than their parents. In today's world, with constant input from television, the internet, and social media, children's inner landscapes are shaped by far more than home life alone. The relationship between parental behaviour and outcomes is not always clear-cut. But that doesn't mean we should ignore the obvious, either.

THE COMPLEXITY OF RESPONSIBILITY

What do we do when a parent says, *I gave them everything they needed to grow up happy and well-adjusted*, but the life of the child tells a different story?

Should we take the parents' word for it? Or trust the outcome? If only it were easy. If only we could assign neat *responsibility percentages*—Parent: 40%. Child: 60%.[16] But human lives don't work like that. Only God can judge situations that complex.

It's enough, perhaps, to acknowledge that most of us give with mixed motives. Very few of us are pure-hearted. Our giving, especially as parents, is often shaped as much by fear as by love. We give because we're afraid of what will happen if we don't. We over-give to control outcomes. We suffer because we can't bear to watch our children suffer.

This was brought home to me during that now-familiar discipline incident with my daughter. I couldn't give her what she wanted—my time, my attention, my patience—and in that moment

I came face to face once again with a painful truth: I am a conditionally loving person.

If children need unconditional love to grow up healthy, then we may all be in trouble.

I don't think I'm unusually selfish or particularly lacking as a parent. But I do know that I have limitations. I've known parents who seem to have a seemingly endless capacity to give, and they are worthy of admiration, not comparison or shame. There is much to learn from them.

And I've known parents who can offer things I simply don't have within me. I cannot pass on ease in a crowd. I cannot pass on light exuberance. I cannot pass on an innate tendency to see the good in everyone.

Becoming the Parent I Wasn't Born to Be

But I can pass on the hard-won lesson of how to see the good in people when it is not one's natural demeanour. I learned this skill partly from books, but also—and perhaps especially— from watching one particular lady who has this quality in abundance and copying her.

I even learned a lot about giving people the benefit of the doubt from another philosophical axiom: Hanlon's Razor. This states that *never attribute to malice that which is adequately explained by stupidity.* Every Christian is familiar with this principle; it's what Jesus did on the cross when he said, *Father, forgive them; they know not what they do* (Luke 23:34). It took me a long time to understand this.

I used to assume that when people had hurt me, they meant to. Now, I realise that most of the time, they didn't. And I've become a much more peaceful and joyful person since understanding that. I'm also a lot nicer to be around. When you stop seeing malice everywhere, you tend to stop spreading it yourself.

Another catchphrase that helped in my struggle to become someone who preferred giving to receiving was *Fake it to make it*. I came across this little gem early in my parenting journey. I knew I'd have to fake the giving thing and hope the reality of becoming a generous person would eventually follow. It was, in many ways, my Christian faith put to the test. If I were supposed to be imitating Christ and growing to resemble him more and more—if prayer really worked, if the sacraments gave grace and changed me—then surely there ought to be results. But what if I didn't change? What if I tried and nothing happened? It was scary to even attempt it.

Of course, my lack of results couldn't disprove the great tenets of the Christian faith. It could simply mean that I was doing something wrong. After all, lots of people have had the experience of praying for something for years and not getting any results, as far as they can tell. But all this time, I had been doing my homework.

I'd already figured out that if you saw God as a great vending machine in the sky and prayed for, say, winning lottery tickets (which I've done), you would likely be disappointed. However, if you prayed fervently for patience, which is a fruit of the Spirit and a great virtue, and you were genuinely willing to let go of your impatience, then patience would surely follow.

How Prayer Changes the Giver

How else are we to make sense of biblical passages where Jesus promises that our heavenly Father knows what we need and will give it to us, even without our prayers (Matt 6: 8)? Or where he promises that God will always answer our prayers (Matt 7: 7). Or the many times where we are assured that prayer untainted by doubt and anger will be answered (Mark 11: 23; Matt 21: 22; 1 Timothy 2: 8)

So I kept praying for the qualities I needed in order to give my children what I presently lacked. I also prayed wholeheartedly for the capacity to keep giving to them at all. Being a parent is tiring nowadays, in ways I am convinced it used not to be.

Plenty of times, I wanted a day off, but I couldn't have it. And in any case, my desire to give to my children exceeded my desire for downtime. I discovered so many prayers that are helpful in this regard. One I loved was the long version of the popular Serenity Prayer:

God grant me the serenity to accept the things I cannot change

The courage to change the things I can

And the wisdom to know the difference.

Grant me patience with the changes that take time

Appreciation of all that I have

Tolerance of those with different struggles

And the strength to get up and try again, one day at a time.

The help I got from this prayer cannot be overstated. In particular, the line about *patience with the changes that take time* comforted me. Since great changes take great lengths of time, transforming me from a self-centred, selfish human being into something more closely resembling Mother Teresa was going to take a while.

In 12-step recovery, we say *we are not saints,* which is usually a reminder to be patient with ourselves—that spiritual progress is the goal, not perfection. But in Christianity, sainthood actually *is* the goal, not in a prideful sense, but as the natural consequence of letting grace do its work. That tension both comforted and challenged me. I was resigned to the idea that it might never happen, but I was also willing to try.

I was greatly impacted by a small booklet containing a lecture Pope St. John Paul II gave to young people, entitled *Don't Be Afraid to be Saints*. It encouraged me to believe that sainthood was the goal, not just for those who seemed born saintly, but for people like me, who were born anything but! It helped me immensely to be regularly reminded that, more than anything, this challenge to love and to give is Christ's great command to us. The whole point of Christianity is to become a saint.

It was also incredibly helpful to keep meditating on the line from the prayer of St. Francis: *It is in giving that we receive.* Because somewhere along the line in my journey from Catholic schoolgirl to atheist mother, I had fully absorbed the world's thinking on this subject. I either gave out of selfish motives, which, as I've suggested, isn't really giving at all, or I experienced giving as diminishing me; I give, you receive. I didn't realise charity was, in fact, reciprocal.

DIVINE LESSONS IN EVERYDAY LIFE

Fortunately, God leaves lessons for us everywhere if you keep your eyes open for them. He helped me learn more about generosity and giving from my children.

When my two were little, birthdays were a very big deal indeed. I recall one year when the present-making for their Dad began at least a month before his birthday, which entailed a lot of cutting and sticking and drawing and decorating and wrapping. In the end, they had created over twenty presents for their Dad.

I watched all this making and doing unfold, marvelled, and delighted in it, at least most of the time. But sometimes, because I'm such a person, I wanted to tell them they had enough presents made already and I wasn't going to buy any more Sellotape. Despite the urge, however, I managed to bite my tongue on these thoughts and headed to the arts and crafts shop. Again.

Because surely it couldn't be right to stifle generosity and their beautiful impulse to give. Their industriousness served to highlight that the children were able to receive by giving. They received hours of amusement, entertainment, and occupation. They received a sense of themselves as competent agents. They received a sense of themselves as loving and caring. They received a sense of connection to their Dad even as he was at work all day while they worked on their gifts, and to me, these seemed to be a worthwhile return for buying unending supplies of tape.

When the presents were finally opened on the day of the birthday, they received joy, delight, happiness, and a sense of being competent and generous. This was receiving by giving in action before my eyes.

And what about their recipient? The children were giving, but was he receiving? Clearly, what they gave their Dad—various and sundry combinations of cardboard, paper, pompoms, glitter, and stickers— had little value, but I will say what he received was *love*. He received *joy*, and these things, of course, are priceless.

My children made it so clear to me that it is in giving that we receive. They also helped me understand I needed to pay careful attention to my motives when I gave gifts.

But not all giving is easy or instinctive. Sometimes we miss the moment entirely—and in doing so, we fail to give what's truly needed.

When We Don't Give What's Needed

One of the great lies of modern parenting is that we have to do it all ourselves. We say we believe it takes a village to raise a child, but we bristle when a teacher corrects our son or when our mother suggests our daughter should say thank you. We've lost something important. In the name of independence or self-expression or rights, we've shut the door on wisdom that used to flow freely between generations, neighbours, teachers, and friends. And now, children are poorly disciplined and parents are frazzled—not because we've failed individually, but because we're no longer allowed to help each other.

I think of an incident from many years ago, when my husband and I failed to give something that was sorely needed. We collected a friend of our son's to take both boys to our daughter's school Christmas fair. The boy came to the door wearing a tiger-print pyjama onesie. He was about ten. It wasn't a costume day, just a normal Saturday event. We were both taken aback, but said nothing. Both of his parents were there. The boy was clearly ready to go. And so we drove off, two children and a tiger in tow.

Our son was mortified. And to be honest, so might we have been if we'd had to hang out with him all day. But more than that, we were confused—not just by the outfit, but by our own inaction. We didn't want to embarrass the boy, offend the parents, or make a scene. Later, we said to each other what we hadn't said at the time: we should have asked him to change. We should have offered him a boundary. We should have offered him the gift of discipline.

But we didn't. And that was our failure, not his.

We decided that if something like that happened again, we'd be brave enough to say, *You're very welcome to come with us, but you need to be dressed.* It's such a small thing, but it matters. That's what discipline is: not punishment, not rejection, but gentle guidance, offered in love. A clear line, kindly given. But these days, even that feels like a risk.

The Cost of Doing Nothing

That boy was a sweet child, clever, musical, and shy. But he was also increasingly shunned by his peers. Our son tried to stay friends, but the lack of basic social skills, including how to dress appropriately, eventually wore thin. Over time, the friendship faded. And I can't help but think that a few well-placed boundaries could have made a world of difference, not just to his social standing, but to his sense of self, of where he fit, and what was expected of him.

In the past, someone might have quietly pulled the child aside. Or had a quiet word with the parents. But now, we say nothing. We don't want to offend, judge, or overstep. So we let children drift into social exclusion, or confusion, or isolation, because we're too afraid to offer what might be received as discipline, even when that discipline is exactly what they need.

Discipline isn't a burden we impose. It's a gift we give. And we don't only give it to our own children. We give it to other people's children, too—or at least, we used to. In doing so, we gave parents support. We helped raise children together. And in turn, we received the peace of knowing we didn't have to do it alone.

Discipline your children, and they will give you peace;
they will bring you the delights you desire. (Proverbs 29:17)

WHAT WE GIVE COMES BACK MULTIPLIED

By now, it's probably clear that I don't believe giving is easy. Or always immediately rewarding. It's often messy, misunderstood, and misfired. Sometimes our giving is mixed with fear, control, or exhaustion. Sometimes we give too much. Sometimes we don't give what is needed at all. And sometimes, we only recognise that in hindsight.

Yet the truth endures: it is in giving that we receive.

Even if we don't do it perfectly, we still grow. Even if our children don't thank us, we are still formed by the effort. Even if the fruit takes years to show—or never appears in the way we imagined—we are changed by the act of offering.

So if you find yourself short on the virtues needed to give well, short on patience, or courage, or generosity, pray. Pray to receive, not so you can store it up, but so you can give it away. Give what you can. Ask for what you lack. And trust that in doing so, you are participating in something much deeper than a transaction or obligation.

You are being formed. You are becoming a saint, slowly and clumsily, perhaps—but surely.

And as it turns out, that's the point. Not to give perfectly, but to be changed in the giving. To receive grace in the very act of trying.

16

It Is in Dying That We Are Born to Eternal Life

I never liked the sound of this line as a girl—there was too much dying in it. As a Christian, I'd been taught about resurrection and heaven, so I understood what it meant. But at that point, I was far too enamoured with specifically *my* life to entertain thoughts that one day I'd die, let alone that this would be a good thing. It seemed a bit morbid, frankly.

By the time I was a teenager, I'd encountered the idea that humans are so frightened of death that we spend much of our lives suppressing its inevitability. Philosophers and psychologists called it *denial*, and while I thought this was probably rubbish, I couldn't ignore the fact that I rarely thought about death, at least not mine. Maybe they were onto something after all.

Still, it's fascinating, isn't it? The brain's ability to tuck such a colossal reality as death away into some dark corner of our consciousness so we can get on with the business of living. Imagine if we could apply that same skill to other worries—our tempers, our resentments, or the maddening tendency to let our egos run the show.

And yet, here's the paradox: while the brain works miracles at hiding death from us, we often let it run wild with fears, anger, and anxiety, wreaking havoc in our lives and relationships. I mean, if my mind is so powerful it can block out the inevitability of my own death, why can't it help me manage my temper enough to avoid snapping at my family? Something isn't adding up here.

And that's where the line from St. Francis begins to make sense—not just in a theological way but in a deeply practical one. To lay down one's life doesn't have to mean literal death. It can mean surrendering the parts of ourselves that are selfish, fearful, or resentful for the sake of others, or even for the sake of a better version of ourselves. In that sense, dying can lead to a new kind of life, one filled with peace, purpose, and love.

But if self-sacrifice leads to life, what happens when a culture turns away from it? When does personal fulfilment take precedence over commitment? Nowhere is this more evident than in our modern attitudes towards marriage and family.

BEHIND THE SMOKE AND MIRRORS OF MODERN PROGRESSIVE THINKING

Divorce is one of the most painful experiences a family can endure, yet society increasingly treats it as inevitable, or even as a positive step in certain cases. Celebrity statements praising former partners, the push to no-fault divorce laws in the name of minimising harm, and a cultural emphasis on emotional well-being all reflect a troubling shift: the idea that personal happiness trumps all other considerations, even the needs of children or the broader fabric of society. Public figures routinely announce their divorces with carefully curated statements about prioritising their children, as though dismantling their family were an act of love rather than loss—a gaslighting of the highest order. Marriage is cast as a private arrangement rather than the cornerstone of a healthy, stable society. In this view, the feelings of adults are paramount, while the long-term impact on children, who often experience divorce as grief, confusion, or even trauma, is too often ignored.

Of course, no one suggests that people should remain in relationships marked by abuse or repeated infidelity. And for many who divorce, the decision is agonising—one they reach only after deep pain and struggle, believing they have exhausted every other option. Yet beneath this experience lies a reality that few are willing to acknowledge: the very fact that divorce is an available path means it is, on some level, seen as legitimate.

A person might insist that they would never have chosen it unless they had no other choice, yet generations before, many would not have seen it as a choice at all. And while the language of *harm reduction* is often used to justify making divorce easier, it rarely acknowledges the deeper harm that divorce itself inflicts, especially on children.

In an age that prizes self-expression and emotional fulfilment, walking away from marriage is now seen, if not as desirable, then at least as permissible—a viable solution when personal happiness is at stake. This mindset could not be further from the idea of self-sacrifice, which lies at the heart of love and family life. Marriage—and especially parenting—requires laying down our own desires and comforts for the sake of another. It demands that we prioritise the well-being of our spouse and children over fleeting emotions or temporary frustrations. True love is not about uninterrupted happiness but about choosing the good of another, even when it costs us something. Or everything.

The Overlooked Victims

It is children who pay the highest price when this sacrificial love is absent. Divorce is rarely just a private matter between two adults. When children are involved, the pain extends far beyond the couple, leaving lasting emotional scars—not just in childhood but for the rest of their lives. This truth, though obvious to many who have lived it, is something society goes to great lengths to deny.

As journalist Bridget Phetasy pointed out in a widely shared article[17], adult children of divorce are often expected to be grateful for their parents' separation and to pretend they are happy about the modern family dynamic even when they are not. Many comply, sensing that their true feelings are unwelcome and that their grief is a burden others would rather not see. It is yet another example of children's needs being made subservient to adults' wants.

At its core, love requires sacrifice. The greatest acts of love always involve setting aside personal desires, frustrations, ambitions, or even life itself for the sake of another. While such selflessness is never easy, it is through these sacrifices that parents grow, not only as individuals but as spiritual beings moving towards sanctification. In choosing to love in this way, we are not merely holding a family together; we are shaping the next generation, teaching by example what it means to be faithful, resilient, and truly human.

But if dying to self brings forth new life, could it be that death itself—our final surrender—also leads to something greater?

We see this pattern everywhere. In nature, seeds must fall to the ground and die before they can bear fruit. In our own lives, every moment of genuine growth requires letting go of something—whether it's selfishness, pride, or comfort—to make room for something greater. Even in marriage and parenting, the deepest joys come not from grasping at happiness but from giving ourselves away in love.

And yet, when it comes to death, the greatest letting go of all, many find it impossible to believe that something greater lies beyond it. Is eternal life just wishful thinking, a story we tell ourselves to soften the blow of mortality? Or is it possible that this pattern of life through death is not just a comforting metaphor but the deepest reality of all?

The Great Debate on Eternal Life

The idea of eternal life has always been a stumbling block for sceptics, who often argue that it's a comforting fairy tale invented to soothe our fear of death. And at first glance, it does sound fantastical. A blissful paradise where we reunite with loved ones and spend eternity with God? For anyone who's spent time navigating the complexities of family relationships, the idea of eternal harmony can seem more like fiction than reality.

But these debates are far from new. Even in Jesus's time, the Sadducees, who rejected the doctrine of the resurrection, couldn't resist mocking the idea. *What about the woman who was married to seven brothers?* They asked. *In the resurrection, whose wife will she be?* You can almost hear their incredulous laughter, as though they had single-handedly dismantled the entire concept of eternal life with one clever question.*

Their scepticism sounds strikingly familiar, doesn't it? Modern doubters often pose similar questions: *How could heaven possibly work with all our messy relationships and tangled histories?* But just as Jesus answered the Sadducees, reminding them that eternal life transcends our limited human understanding, these questions today reflect more about our assumptions than about the plausibility of resurrection. Others dismiss the idea of heaven as tedious—an endless, unchanging harmony that sounds more dull than rewarding. But perhaps this, too, reveals more about our earthly limitations than about the reality of eternal life. What if true harmony isn't stagnation but the deepest fulfilment, a joy so complete that we can scarcely imagine it from our current vantage point?

And despite the denial, our longing for eternal life persists—not just in Christianity but across cultures and belief systems. Even

* Matthew 22: 23-33; Mark 12: 18-27; Luke 20: 27-40

as secular materialism grows, the idea of reincarnation has gained ground, and it's striking how rarely this belief is dismissed as wishful thinking. Perhaps that's because, deep down, we all sense that life cannot simply end. Our desire to reconnect with lost loved ones, to see wrongs made right, and to find peace beyond this world points to something greater.

Christianity's promise of eternal life is more than just a balm for grief. It's an invitation to live differently here and now. To embrace the idea of resurrection is to recognise that our lives on earth have meaning beyond themselves. It's hard to believe that how we live and what we sacrifice for others matters eternally.

This is where the idea of *dying to self* becomes crucial. To live for others, to lay down one's life in love and service, is to participate in the promise of eternal life. Whether that means raising children with patience and devotion, forgiving those who've hurt us, or putting aside personal desires for the sake of the greater good, each act of selflessness becomes a small reflection of the resurrection we hope for.

Of course, there are questions about heaven, purgatory, and hell, about who will be there and what it will look like. But these details, fascinating as they are, pale in comparison to the central truth: eternal life is not just a distant hope; it's a reality we are called to prepare for, starting today.

WHEN CHILDREN ASK ABOUT DEATH

At a recent recovery book club, where we gather for a potluck supper and discussion on a spiritual theme, one of the members—a young mum in recovery, just a few years sober—shared a story that stayed with me. Her four-year-old daughter had begun to ask about death, specifically about whether her mummy would die and when.

This mum, shocked and unprepared for such a profound question from someone so young, struggled to respond. From her materialist perspective, she didn't believe in an afterlife, and she was determined not to lie to her daughter. She offered what reassurance she could: that, hopefully, her death was a long way off. But beyond that, she had nothing to give.

As I listened, my heart broke for both of them. This little girl, grappling with one of life's deepest mysteries, was met with a well-meaning but incomplete answer. She needed more than just the hope that death was far away—she needed to know that death isn't the end of the story and that the love she shares with her mother isn't bound by time or space but will endure beyond this life.

What struck me most is how widespread this experience is. From my private practice, I know that children often start asking these kinds of questions at a young age, long before many adults think they're capable of such existential curiosity. And in the rooms of 12-step recovery, I've heard countless people share how they themselves grappled with these questions as children, often thinking they were alone in wondering about life, death, and what comes after.

Yet, how often do we underestimate children's capacity to wonder about life and death? How often do we delude ourselves into thinking they aren't wondering about these questions simply because they don't express them in words?

That night, I couldn't help but think how different it would have been if this mum had faith—faith in an afterlife, in heaven, in a God who holds all of us, including her and her daughter, in eternal love. With faith, she could have offered her daughter not just reassurance about the distant future but a greater truth: that death is not the end, that they will one day be reunited in heaven, and that love is never truly lost.

For me, this story isn't just about a parent struggling to answer a difficult question. It's also about the profound human need for hope in something greater than this life. It's a need that points, I believe, to the truth of the resurrection. After all, why would we long so deeply for eternal connection if it weren't part of the design of our being?

WHAT WE BELIEVE DOESN'T CHANGE WHAT IS

Listening to that young mum at the Step 11 book club made me think about how often we mistake our doubts for truth. Her materialist perspective didn't allow her to offer her daughter the comfort of hope in eternal life, but that didn't make eternal life any less real, just unavailable to her at that moment.

This is the thing about truth: it doesn't need our belief to exist. I may not believe that 1 + 1 = 2, but that's my problem, not mathematics'. Similarly, all the people who don't believe in God don't stop him from being true. So even though the resurrection might be hard to get your head around, that's not going to stop it from happening. Unless, of course, the Church is wrong about that.

Here's the thing: as a Catholic, I've come to accept that what the Church teaches on faith and morals is always infallibly correct. I know that's a bold claim, and it's one I wrestled with myself for years. For many readers, it may feel like an insurmountable leap of faith. But for me, it became clear that either the Church is entirely trustworthy in these matters, or it isn't. I couldn't pick and choose which parts of the Creed to believe without undermining the whole.

As I returned to Christianity after years of detours through nihilism, paganism, agnosticism, and even atheism, I found myself starting to believe in the major tenets of Christianity in the order they appear in the Creed.

First, my faith in God returned. I stayed there quite happily for a long time, blissfully unaware that I'd taken only the first step on the rollercoaster ride God was about to take me on. Next came God as Father, the maker of heaven and earth, of all things seen and unseen (or visible and invisible, as we say today).

Then came the shocking, dawning realisation that I believed in Jesus as the Son of God. And so it went, down through the lines of the Creed, until I got stuck at the resurrection and eternal life. Eventually, I figured out that while I couldn't yet make myself believe this part, it didn't make sense to reject it. Instead, I trusted that my belief would follow in God's time.

THE LOGIC OF LIFE AFTER DEATH

At some point, eternal life after death may become scientifically undeniable, or mostly undeniable, at least, since people are capable of denying anything if they insist on doing so. But in the absence of definitive proof, logic can already lead us there.

Take eyes, for example. Eyes are perfectly evolved to see, which presupposes that there are things to see and light to illuminate them. If you are a creature living at the bottom of the ocean, where there's no light and nothing to see, you don't have eyes, because there's no point in having them.*

Or consider wisdom teeth. Once essential for chewing tough, raw food, they've become unnecessary as humans discovered fire and invented cooking. Over time, we've started evolving them out—some people already have fewer than four, and eventually, no one will have them. Nature doesn't waste energy on things that serve no purpose.

And this brings us to eternal life. Human beings have an undeniable longing for something beyond this world, for permanence, connection, and meaning that transcends the temporary. If our needs are so often met by the realities of the world around us, why would this deepest longing—our desire for eternity—be the exception?

God doesn't waste. He doesn't create without purpose or equip us with things we don't need. And if he's placed the yearning for eternal life within us, doesn't it follow that eternal life exists? Our very longing points to the beautiful logic of a divinely ordered

* Some deep-sea creatures, rather than losing their eyes, develop exceptionally large and sensitive ones to detect even the faintest traces of bioluminescence. However, in environments of total darkness, the more common adaptation is to dispense with eyes entirely.

universe—a universe in which nothing, and certainly not love, is wasted.

Our Deepest Longing

Let's turn now to parenthood and how all the ideas we've discussed thread into its complex universe. I've yet to meet a parent who isn't shattered by the thought of losing their child. It's the worst thing in the world for a child to die before their parent—a universal agreement, I think.

It's equally tragic for a child to lose a parent. Several years ago, my community in Guildford was rocked by a brutal murder. A father was stabbed to death in front of his fourteen-year-old son within minutes of getting onto a train into London.

People talked about it, posted about it, and prayed about it. Everyone, absolutely everyone, agreed it was a shockingly terrible thing for that boy to have experienced. His father died in his arms—an awful reality to contemplate, and not least because my own son was also fourteen at the time.

I kept thinking about how easily it could have been my husband and son heading to London for a father-and-son day out. And yet, in an instant, this father was gone, killed by a stranger in a fit of murderous rage.

I didn't know if this family believed in eternal life, but I hoped they did. I didn't know if the man's parents were still alive, but as he was only fifty-one, it was plausible. The absolute need for parents to believe they will someday see a child again in heaven is, for me, the best proof of eternal life. If there were no heaven, why would we have such a profound longing for reunion?

As a parent, I couldn't help but wonder: *Has this boy stopped crying yet?* I knew there would be moments of respite, even in those early days of grief. Or perhaps he hadn't cried at all—shocked and numb, which was unlikely but possible.

Murder is truly an act that rips at the fabric of our world. It's the first *Thou shalt not* commandment because it's so essential to live rightly and not murder our fellow human beings. Yet, even in the first generation of humanity, sibling rivalry tipped over into murder.

The story of Cain and Abel reveals perennial truths about the darker sides of human nature—jealousy, rage, and revenge. Any parent with more than one child has likely witnessed sibling rivalry, albeit far short of these biblical brothers, but the tendency is undeniable.

Still, we long for something better. For a world where sorrow has been wiped away, where the lion lies down with the lamb.

Many who reject God do so because they long for this perfect harmony and believe it's more achievable without religion.

But this longing for a world without death and suffering, for reunion with those we love, isn't wishful thinking. God would not equip us with such a need if he didn't intend to fulfil it. The desire of every grieving parent to see their child again is, for me, proof of heaven. And not for the first time, my experience of being a parent has led me to a deep, unshakeable belief in a tenet of Christianity that, at first, seemed incomprehensible or unnecessary but now makes perfect sense.

Dying to Self and Living for Others

Throughout this chapter, I've focused on literal death and the promise of eternal life. But there's another way to understand the St. Francis prayer: in dying to self, we awaken to a new kind of life, here and now.

In the Alcoholics Anonymous text, *The Twelve Steps and Twelve Traditions,* the line from the prayer is rendered, "It is in dying that we awaken to eternal life." The sung version I love says, "It is…in dying that we're born to eternal life." Whichever way you phrase it, the idea that spiritual growth requires some form of dying and rebirth while still alive is a universal truth.

The apostle Paul speaks of being *dead to sin and alive in Christ* (Romans 6:11). Born-again Christians emphasise the necessity of rebirth during this life, participating in Christ's death and resurrection to become new creations. In psychological terms, it's about reducing the grip of the ego. In Eastern philosophies, it's about realising that the self is an illusion and letting go of attachment to it. Across traditions, spiritual awakening demands that some part of us die to make way for new life.

Even in secular culture, we see echoes of this idea. Our modern use of the word *woke* stems from the notion of having *awakened* to systemic injustice, social inequalities, or ingrained cultural blind spots that were previously unseen. To be woke, in its original sense, is to have gone through a kind of death of ignorance or complacency in order to live more consciously.

The principle is the same in recovery: real transformation involves a dying of the old self. The antidote to self-centredness is reaching out to others, developing an interest in how we can serve someone other than ourselves. The process also requires uncovering the parts of ourselves that need to die in order to become the people God intends us to be.

Speaking from experience, I've found that my arrogance, judgmentalism, pride, cynicism, superiority, inferiority, gluttony, anger, despair, procrastination, lack of charity, selfishness, unforgiveness, shame, and self-hatred all had to die. There are surely more I've forgotten—and there are parts of me that still need to be put to death daily. It hasn't been exhaustive, but it's been a good start. I hope my husband and children will agree.

The Gift of Eternal Life, Here and Now

As I said at the beginning of this book, God inserted himself into my life of desolation and selfishness almost two decades ago and set me on a new path. It's been a tremendous adventure ever since, and today, I live a life beyond my wildest dreams.

This new life, which I now understand is the start of my eternal life, feels so precious, so abounding in love and peace, that there are times when I can hardly believe my luck. Jesus said he came so that we might have life and have it to the full. Having traversed the tumultuous journey of finding faith, I now know what he meant.

I once was lost, but now I am found. I was blind, but now I see. Plenty of times, I've felt like the woman weeping at Jesus's feet, covering them with precious ointment and tears. I know now that this is what it feels like to love and be loved. This is what it feels like to be free.

St Irenaeus wrote *Gloria Dei est vivens homo* (the glory of God is man fully alive), and in my experience, there are moments when I feel so alive, so joyful and grateful to God, that I could die and go to heaven right now, knowing everything has turned out okay. But God clearly has different plans for me because here I am—just for today, I am still alive, still practising the spiritual principles he's teaching me, and still preparing for eternity.

I can hardly wait.

EPILOGUE

A Heart in Progress

It turns out God is far more patient than I am. He has had to be. I once had a heart that was closed in on itself—too fearful to trust, too wounded to love fully. But God, in his infinite mercy, did not leave me there. He took my shrivelled heart and, over the years, gently stretched it. Through grace, through suffering, through the daily work of showing up for my family, my faith, and my recovery, he expanded my heart so that I might love more—more freely, more generously, more completely.

Perhaps your journey has been different. Or perhaps, in some way, it has been the same. Maybe you, too, have found yourself struggling to trust, reluctant to repair, fearful of the cost of love. Maybe you have discovered, as I have, that peace is not the absence of struggle, nor is love the absence of irritation (as any married person or parent will confirm).

If this journey has taught me anything, it is that love is not something we simply feel. It is something we choose again and again, often in the quiet, unremarkable moments that shape a life.

Love lets go of a grudge when hurt, rather than clinging to it. Love chooses peace when conflict would be easier. Love shows up, even when the other person is being spectacularly unreasonable. (And yes, sometimes that other person is me.)

I have learned, slowly and imperfectly, that peace is not the absence of struggle, nor is love the absence of difficulty. Through all the ups and downs, God has expanded my heart in ways I never imagined. The work is not done—if anything, I suspect he has quite a bit left to do—but now I trust that he will finish what he started.

So if my heart was once shrivelled, perhaps it is now… less so. A heart in progress or a work under construction, if you may. And thankfully, God does not require perfection—only willingness.

If this book has been about anything, it has been about that willingness, the willingness to love and to seek peace. To repair what has been broken. To show up even when it is hard. To trust that no matter how much work remains, the One who began it in me will bring it to completion

ACKNOWLEDGEMENTS

I would like to begin by thanking my family of origin—my parents, my siblings, and the wider clan I was born into. My roots run deep in that soil. I am grateful for everything I received from them and for the foundation they laid in me.

To all those who taught me, both formally and informally, I extend my sincere thanks. My undergraduate and postgraduate years in psychology and theology were shaped by many fine minds, but the influence of those I've read, worked with, studied under, and learned from across the years extends far beyond the classroom. Even those not mentioned by name are woven into the fabric of this book, their insights echoing in its pages. I also wish to note that I take full responsibility for any errors in these pages and absolve my teachers of any responsibility for my inaccuracies and misunderstandings.

To my recovery family—my fellows in the rooms of the many 12-step programmes I've attended over the years—I owe a debt I could never repay. Thank you for your honesty, your courage, and your companionship on this path of sanity and grace. I also honour the founders of Alcoholics Anonymous, Dr Bob and Bill W. Recovery gave me my life back. As the Big Book so perfectly puts it: I used to thank Alcoholics Anonymous for putting God in my life; now I thank God for putting Alcoholics Anonymous in my life.

To my sponsors, past and present, thank you for your wisdom, your guidance, and your love. In particular, I want to thank Mary, my current sponsor, who has walked with me through more than a dozen years of the strange and sacred symmetry of learning the same lessons at the same time. She knows I see her as a gift in my life, and I remain endlessly grateful for the experience, strength, and hope we continue to share. I also want to acknowledge my sponsees, from whom I have learned just as much, if not more.

To my husband, the love of my life, and to our two beautiful children, thank you. You are among the greatest gifts I have ever been given. This book would not exist without you. While it is my memoir, it is also your story. I am so grateful that you allowed me to tell it. Your presence in these pages gives them life, and your willingness to let me write from the heart has been an act of generosity and trust that moves me deeply. I love you more than I can say.

And finally, my thanks go to my Higher Power—God, as I have come to know him through recovery, through Scripture, and through the Church. The God of the Bible, Father, Son, and Holy Spirit. It was you who nudged me to write this book, and I hope I have done you justice. Thank you for the incomparable gift of faith—my truest anchor and the quiet thread running through every chapter of my life. As Thomas Merton once prayed, I do not know if I am doing your will, but I know that the desire to please you does in fact please you. Thank you for the healing. But above all, thank you for helping me to know, deep in my soul, that I am your beloved.

ABOUT THE AUTHOR

Samantha Duggan is a behavioural psychologist, writer, Catholic mother of two, and woman in long-term 12-step recovery. She has a PhD in Clinical Neuropsychology from the University of St Andrews, Scotland and an MA in Christian Spirituality from St Mary's University, Twickenham. She works and writes at the intersection of psychology and spirituality, with a particular focus on family life, emotional sobriety, and the pursuit of peace in ordinary moments. She lives with her husband, children, cat and dog in Surrey. *Channels of Peace* is her first book.

SELECTED BIBLIOGRAPHY

The books listed below are a partial selection from the titles referenced throughout the text and are recommended for further reading.

Brené Brown. *Daring Greatly: How the Courage to Be Vulnerable Transforms the Way We Live, Love, Parent, and Lead.* Avery, 2012.

Deepak Chopra. *The Seven Spiritual Laws of Success: A Practical Guide to the Fulfillment of Your Dreams.* Amber-Allen Publishing, 1994.

Henry Cloud and John Townsend. *Boundaries with Kids: When to Say Yes, How to Say No.* Zondervan, 1998.

Adele Faber and Elaine Mazlish. *How to Talk So Kids Will Listen & Listen So Kids Will Talk.* Scribner, 1980.

Dr Becky Kennedy. *Good Inside: A Guide to Becoming the Parent You Want to Be.* Harper Wave, 2022.

Gabor Maté and Gordon Neufeld. *Hold On to Your Kids: Why Parents Need to Matter More Than Peers.* Ballantine Books, 2004.

Henri Nouwen. *Life of the Beloved: Spiritual Living in a Secular World.* Crossroad Publishing, 1992.

Timothy Radcliffe. *What Is the Point of Being a Christian?* Burns & Oates, 2005.

Marshall B. Rosenberg. *Nonviolent Communication: A Language of Life.* 3rd ed., PuddleDancer Press, 2015.

Richard C. Schwartz. *Introduction to the Internal Family Systems Model.* Trailheads Publications, 2001.

Sister Stanislaus Kennedy. *Gardening the Soul: A Spiritual Daybook.* Transworld Ireland, 2002.

Saint Pope John Paul II. *Do Not Be Afraid to Be Saints: Message of John Paul II to Young People.* Veritas Publications, 2000.

REFERENCES

1 Lee, B., & Lee, B. (2022, April 7). The Problem with Parental Favoritism - The Survey Center on American Life. The Survey Center on American Life - A nonprofit organization dedicated to understanding the way cultural, political, and technological changes are shaping the lives of ordinary Americans. https://www.americansurveycenter.org/the-problem-with-parental-favoritism/?utm_source=chatgpt.com

2 Neff, K., & Germer, C. (2017). *Self-compassion and psychological well-being.* In E. M. Seppälä, E. Simon-Thomas, S. L. Brown, M. C. Worline, C. D. Cameron, & J. R. Doty (Eds.), *The Oxford Handbook of Compassion Science* (pp. 371–385). Oxford University Press.

3 Harvard Health. (2021, February 12). *The power of forgiveness.* https://www.health.harvard.edu/mind-and-mood/the-power-of-forgiveness?utm_source=chatgpt.com

4 England, M. J., & Sim, L. J. (2009). *Associations between depression in parents and parenting, child health, and child psychological functioning.* Depression in Parents, Parenting, and Children - NCBI Bookshelf. https://www.ncbi.nlm.nih.gov/books/NBK215128/

5 Szurek-Cabanas, R., Navarro-Carrillo, G., Martínez-Sánchez, C. A., Oyanedel, J. C., & Villalobos, D. (2024). *Socioeconomic status and maternal postpartum depression: a PRISMA-compliant systematic review.* Current Psychology, 1-12.

6 *All about emotional tears.* (2017, February 28). American Academy of Ophthalmology. https://www.aao.org/eye-health/tips-prevention/all-about-emotional-tears

7 Collier, L. *Why we cry.* https://www.apa.org. https://www.apa.org/monitor/2014/02/cry

8 Brown, B. (2012). *Men, women and worthiness: The experience of shame and the power of being enough.* [Audio CD] Sounds True.

9 Herrando, C., & Constantinides, E. (2021). *Emotional Contagion: A Brief Overview and Future Directions.* Frontiers in Psychology, 12, Article 712606. https://doi.org/10.3389/fpsyg.2021.712606

10 Kirsch, I., Deacon, B. J., Huedo-Medina, T. B., Scoboria, A., Moore, T. J., & Johnson, B. T. (2008). *Initial severity and antidepressant benefits: A meta-analysis of data submitted to the Food and Drug Administration.* PLOS Medicine, 5(2), e45.

11 Lu, C. Y., & Zhang, F. (2014). *Antidepressants' black-box warning — 10 years later.* The New England Journal of Medicine, 371(18), 1666–1668. https://doi.org/10.1056/NEJMp1408480

12 Nelson, C. A., Fox, N. A., & Zeanah, C. H. (2014). *Romania's Abandoned Children: Deprivation, Brain Development, and the Struggle for Recovery.* Harvard University Press.

13 Imuta, K., Henry, J. D., Slaughter, V., Selcuk, B., & Ruffman, T. (2016). *Theory of mind, empathy, and prosocial behavior in children and adolescents: A meta-analysis.* Developmental Psychology, 52(8), 1192-1205. doi:10.1037/dev0000140

14 Centers for Disease Control and Prevention. (2023). *Teen mental health study reveals disconnect with parents.* Parents.com. Retrieved from https://www.parents.com/teen-mental-health-study-reveals-disconnect-with-parents-8680260.

15 Maccoby, E. E., & Martin, J. A. (1983). *Socialization in the context of the family: Parent-child interaction.* In P. H. Mussen (ED.), *Handbook of Child Psychology* (Vol. 4, pp. 1-101). New York: Wiley

16 Cloud, H.& Townsend, J. S. (2001). *Boundaries with kids: How healthy choices grow healthy children.* Zondervan.

17 Phetasy, B. https://thespectator.com/topic/how-divorce-never-ends/

Printed in Great Britain
by Amazon

62414463R00184